A Persian Cookbook:
The Manual

A Persian Cookbook: The Manual

A 16th century Persian cookbook by Bavarchi

Translated from the Persian by
Saman Hassibi & Amir Sayadabdi

PROSPECT BOOKS
2018

This edition published in 2018 by Prospect Books at 26 Parke Road, London, SW13 9NG

British Library Cataloguing in Publication Data:
A catalogue entry for this book is available from the British Library.

ISBN 978-1-909248-59-5

Set in Adobe Garamond Pro and Cochin by Catheryn Kilgarriff and Brendan King.

Printed by the Gutenberg Press Ltd., Malta.

Contents

Contents

Contents

Translators' Introduction

This book is a translation of the earliest classical cookbook in Persian to have survived, titled *Kār-nāme* (*The Manual*). *The Manual* was drafted in 1521 by *Hāji Mohammad Ali Bāvarči Baqdādi* (hereafter Bavarchi), after a spiritual pilgrimage to Ardabil to see the shrines of two prominent figures of the Safavids, *Šeix Safi-addin-e Ardabili* and *Šeix Haydar*. Upon his return, Bavarchi felt obligated to present his patron with a gift as a token of appreciation. Being a professional cook, Bavarchi decided that compiling a manuscript on 'cooking and its craft' would be a gift befitting the high station of his patron, as 'no one had ever compiled such a work before and no one had ever been in possession of one'.

The manuscript does not reveal much about the life of Bavarchi, except that he was a professional cook, as was his late father. In fact, this is obvious in his title, as *bāvarči* literally means 'cook' in Persian. His father was a professional cook for the late '*Mirzā Budāq*' who appears to be, judging from his title, a member of the royalty or aristocracy. Bavarchi himself also cooked for an aristocratic patron, though he refers to him only as '*Mirzā'i*', making the pinpointing of the patron's identity difficult, if not impossible.

In keeping with the conventions of the time, Bavarchi begins the manuscript by praising God and the prophet Mohammad, followed by an ornate and exquisite praise of his patron, as well as Shah Ismail I – the founder of the Safavid dynasty – during whose reign the manuscript was written. He also notes that what he is going to present in the manuscript is not based merely on his own experience and initiative, but also on what he has read in the books of intellectuals and learnt from the master chefs of the time.

Recipes in *The Manual* are relatively consistent in terms of giving details as to the methods of preparation, ingredients and measurement. This is in contrast with the other cookbook that has survived from the Safavid era (1597) entitled *Māddat-ol hayāt* (*The Substance of Life*), which gives, at times, very general and cursory descriptions without presenting the method of preparation or even the required ingredients. *The Manual*, in this respect, is very similar to modern cookbooks.

Although Bavarchi claims in his preface that *The Manual* is written for the benefit of the commoner as well as the nobility, his recipes often call for large quantities and a multiplicity of ingredients, and demand the use of some elaborate techniques and luxury foodstuffs which would probably not have been accessible, at least in those quantities, to the lower class. This suggests that the elaborate stews and extravagant pilafs found in *The Manual* were most likely prepared for large aristocratic households. However, there are, at times, recipes for modest pilafs and simple soups, and porridges made with ingredients that were more likely to be expected in the diet of the ordinary people, suggesting that these dishes might have been inspired by the cuisine of the lower social classes. *The Manual* therefore provides not only an insight into Persian haute cuisine of the early sixteenth century, but also a glimpse into what ordinary people ate at the time.

The importance of *The Manual* does not lie merely in providing a background to the Middle Eastern and Persian cuisine and food culture. *The Manual* was written during one of the greatest post-Islam eras of Persia. Safavid Persia (1501-1736) was vast, stretching approximately from today's Afghanistan to Georgia, with international trade ties. Within *The Manual* there are dishes named after locations and cities that are outside the borders of today's Iran. In these recipes, implications of racial and ethnic differentiations in the Middle and Near East are found, making *The Manual* a document that depicts the historical reality of the people who created, cooked, and ate these dishes, laying new ground for the cultural historian.

Translators' Introduction

As many culinary historians have noted, the lack of translated resources is one of the main obstacles in globalizing the field of culinary history. This lack of translated works is felt even more greatly when it comes to the Middle East, particularly Iran, where some of the most influential culinary traditions and significant foods were born, yet to date there is only one complete English translation of a historical Iranian cookbook.[1] Therefore, we hope that this book speaks to English-speaking food enthusiasts as well as culinary historians and food scholars. We envisage that this book will be able to provide an objective narration of Persian food culture and the food culture of Iranians, and contribute to the revival of dishes, customs, and culinary heritage that have already disappeared or fallen into decline.

About the Manuscript

The complete title of the manuscript, as given by Bavarchi in his opening page, is *The Manual on Cooking and its Craft*. The author initially states in his introduction that the book consists of twenty-six chapters; however, there are only twenty-four chapters in the list of contents he provides, and the final manuscript contains only twenty-two chapters. Apart from the missing chapters in the text, there are also some inconsistencies between the chapter titles given in the introduction and those in the book itself.

The sole manuscript of *The Manual* that has survived is held at the Central Library of the University of Tehran, Iran. The manuscript has 103 pages, with each page consisting of eleven lines written in *Nasx* (*Naskh*) script in black ink, with the titles written in red ink.

The whole text is in Persian, apart from a few clauses or phrases – mostly complimentary or prayer – that are in Arabic. There are a few words that are illegible or missing, and in these instances we have added our own words in square brackets [ ]. Words within brackets are also used in cases where the literal translation would have resulted in too much vagueness and made the instructions hard to follow.

1. *Dining at the Safavid Court*, a translation of *Māddat-ol hayāt* by M. R. Ghanoonparvar, Mazda Publishers.

Parentheses ( ) are used wherever particular utensils or kitchenware were mentioned. The names of these tools were translated to their modern equivalent for ease of reading, but their Persian names are presented between parentheses, e.g. 'pan' (*komājdān*). A full list of equipment can be found in Table One. Words in parenthesis may also communicate implied meanings in recipes: e.g. 'stuff it (hen)' or 'pound the meat (to form meatballs)'. Finally, there are terms that in different contexts bear different meanings; for instance a term such as '*qeyme*' can be translated as 'to dice', 'diced', 'meat base for some soups', 'filling or stuffing' or 'fried, diced meat', depending on the context. On such occasions, we have included the Persian word in parenthesis after the word. '*Kufte*', '*havāej*', '*masāleh*' and '*qaliye*' are other examples of this kind.

The Romanization of words, including Arabic or Turkish loan words, is based on the Persian pronunciation of the words, and is cross-checked with the most extensive dictionary of Persian language, the Dehkhoda dictionary. See Table Four.

Recipe Terminology & Batterie de Cuisine

Although this manuscript belongs to the early sixteenth century, the recipes are remarkably detailed; they generally include explicit instructions as well as precise measurements. Still, there are times when the instructions may be rather ambiguous. On such occasions, we have provided a little more context for readers who may not be too familiar with the classic Persian culinary repertoire.

Hot or warm descriptions do not necessarily refer to the heat (i.e. spiciness) of the ingredients, but to their inherent properties and temperaments, and their corresponding humours. According to the Humoral System – that is still extremely popular in Iran and has greatly influenced Iranian cuisine – the four temperaments of foodstuffs (warm, cold, wet, and dry) should be combined in such a way as to restore the balance of the foods and therefore the body. For instance the warmness of a particular ingredient should be neutralized by the coldness of another, and so on. Therefore the term 'warm spices' has been used when translating '*adviye-ye garm*', as the word '*garm*' refers to the humour of the spices and not the spiciness (i.e. hotness) of the spices. This is essentially the idea behind subcontinental Indian garam masala; however, the palates and therefore the mixture of Persian warm spices and Indian garam masala vary vastly.

The word '*āb*' literally translates to 'water'; however, in some recipes '*āb*' was used as a short form of '*āb-e gušt*' which is equivalent to 'meat broth'. In such cases, we translated the word contextually. At times, *āb* was also used to make compound nouns, in which case we translated it to 'soup'. For instance, *noxodāb* (Chapter Five), is from *noxod* (chickpea) and *āb* (water), which translated to 'chickpea soup'. We also translated the term '*šarbat-āb dādan*' to 'drizzle water' or 'spoon water', because although '*šarbat*' can be translated to 'syrup', it was not implied, in this text, that a sort of syrup was to be added. This becomes clearer if we note that whenever any type of flavouring (sugar, honey, etc.) was to be added, the author diligently and explicitly named them and explained how and when they should be added.

In a typical recipe that uses sliced, diced, or chopped meat, it is the common practice for the author to 'remove the foam'. '*Kaf*' in Persian literally translates to 'foam' in English. Although the term could also be translated as 'scum', we deliberately decided to use the word 'foam' as the latter is more inclusive. 'Froth' was used in only one recipe (*kallemāčān* in Chapter Twelve), in which the author's instruction was to 'skim off the layer of fat froth' which was to be *kept* and *used*, as opposed to foam which must be *removed* and *discarded*.

At times, numbers are part of the verb. For instance, '*yek juš zadan*' (literally: to boil once), indicates that the ingredient must be boiled only for a little while. In these instances, the numbers were not translated literally. Thus, '*yek juš zadan*' (literally: to boil once) has been translated to 'to boil for a moment', '*do juš zadan*' (literally: to boil twice) to 'to boil for a few moments', and '*čand juš zadan*' (literally: to boil a few times) to 'to boil for some moments'. '*Yek čarx dādan*' (literally: to stir once) has been translated to 'to sauté' as they both mean shallow-frying for a short period of time.

As the word '*sāati*' does not provide a known and measured amount of time (although '*saat*' literally means 'hour'), it has been translated to 'awhile' to carry over the ambiguity of the original manuscript into its English translation.

Āš: (*aash*) is a thick soup or stew with legumes, grains or noodles, vegetables and sometimes meat, and is a significant dish in Iranian cuisine, so much so that the Persian words for cookery/cuisine (*āšpazi*), cook (*āšpaz*) and kitchen (*āšpaz-xāne*) are all derived from *āš*. Although in today's Iran *āš* has become a generic term for any thick soup regardless of its ingredients and preparation methods, Bavarchi categorized *āš* in three different chapters: Chapter Two (with noodles), Chapter Three (with grains), and Chapter Seven (sour tasting).

A close investigation of the text reveals the difference between these types of *āš*. Noodle *āš* (Chapter Two) has a meat base, to which vegetables and then noodles are added, and is served with different toppings and condiments (*qāteq*[2]) that are to be added either after the dish is served or during the final steps of cooking. To grain *āš* (Chapter Three) with wheat or barley, no topping is added; however, it might be flavoured to taste. Sour *āš* (Chapter Seven) is cooked in sour liquid or is flavoured with fruit pastes while cooking, and is complemented at the end by minced garlic or dried mint and sometimes sugar to balance the taste and humours.

Grain *āš* recipes may also seem quite similar to *harise* (harissa) recipes (Chapter Eight), especially barley and wheat harissa; however, the main distinction between the two lies in the fact that harissa recipes call only for meat and grains whereas *āš* recipes demand legumes and vegetables as well. Also, unlike *āš*, harissa is served with toppings of warmed mutton tallow, with ground sugar and cinnamon.

Recipes for *šurbā* (Chapter Four) and *māstbā* (Chapter Six) are also very similar to those of *āš*. In fact, dictionaries present *āš* to be a synonym to the Middle-Persian *bā* (meaning stew, gruel or thick soup) that is usually used as a suffix to form dish names. For instance, the word *šurbā* is made from *šur* (salty, savoury) and *bā*, meaning 'savoury *āš*'; similarly, the word *māstbā* consists of *māst* (yogurt) and

2. *Katex* in Persian (condiments for *āš*), not to be confused with *qāteq* (Turkish, *katax* in Persian) – a type of fermented yogurt similar to *kašk* – the former is a general term while the latter is a particular type of condiment/ingredient.

bā, meaning 'yogurt *āš*'.[3] However, Bavarchi presents neither *šurbā* nor *māstbā* under the heading of *āš*, but within their independent chapters; there are some differences in the preparation methods and ingredients used in *āš* as opposed to those of *šurbā* and *māstbā*, but the main distinction may be that *šurbā* recipes always call for rice, meat, vegetables and legumes, while *āš* recipes never call for any rice.

Meat: The most common meat that has been used in this manuscript is mutton, hogget, or lamb. There are a few vegetarian dishes and one vegan dish in the text and there are two dishes in which fish has been used. Hens and gamebirds are also widely used.

There are times when it is directed that the meat be cooked until it becomes '*moharrā*'. This term has been translated to 'fall-apart tender' as it is from the Arabic '*tahrae*', meaning the food should be cooked thoroughly until the meat becomes very tender, or cooked until the meat falls off the bone.

When the recipes use tripe – usually sheep's or lamb's – we have used flat tripe instead of *rumen*, reed tripe instead of *abomasum*, and book tripe instead of *omasum*.

Rice: In many recipes in which rice is used, the author's instructions included pounding the rice with salt, which is then sieved, washed and used. This is the process of milling the rice and discarding the husk. 'Whitening the rice' refers to milling and polishing the grains to remove any remaining germ or husk from the grains – which seems redundant in today's world.

There are three main types of dish that are made with rice: various forms of *palaw* (Chapters Nine, Eleven, Twelve, and Thirteen), *šilepalaw* (Chapter Ten), and *šurbā* (Chapter Four). *Palaw* (*polo* in today's Persian and pilaf in English) is rice that is stuffed with other ingredients and different types of it are described in this book. There

3. Examples of the suffix '*bā*' (or *bāg*) can also be found in the eleventh-century text of *Ibn Sayyar al-Warraq* and the thirteenth-century of *Al-Baghdadi,* both of which are filled with recipes bearing Persian names. For instance *zirbāj, Al-sikbāj, nirbāj,* etc. are all two-word compounds with their first element being the Persian name of their main ingredient (*zir=zire*=cumin; *sik=sek*=vinegar; *nir=nār*=pomegranate) and their second element the suffix *bāj* (the Arabicized form of *bāg*), making them cumin stew, vinegar stew, and pomegranate stew. Interestingly, an almost-identical recipe to *Al Baghdadi's Al-sikbāj* is called *'āš-e serke'* (vinegar stew) in Bavarchi's manuscript (Chapter Seven).

is the chapter for *palawdāne* (grainy pilaf) which emphasizes the grainy texture that any good Persian pilaf must have. Although this point is not particularly made in other *palaw* chapters, nonetheless the instructions are suitable to make pilafs with separate grains. This type of dish is perhaps the inspiration to *al-Baghdadi's āruzz mufalfal* as suggested by Charles Perry.

Šilepalaw, however, is from '*šile*' (or *šole*; literally soft, watery) and *palaw* (pilaf). In the instructions for this sort of dish, quite opposite to the instructions for pilaf, the author made a particular point by stating that 'having absorbed the water and oil, the rice blossoms'. This description refers to the point where rice grains have been cooked for a longer than usual time and are opening up (i.e. losing their shape). Therefore, the texture for *šilepalaw* is closer to sticky rice – yet it is perhaps drier than *šurbā* (see above).

Grains: Wheat, barley, and rice were used in making different types of soups (*āš* and *šurbā*) and harissa (*harise*). Although harissa is known as *halim* in today's Iran, they are, in this text, two different things. *Harise* has been used by Bavarchi as the generic term for the dishes that are porridge-like and include some form of meat. *Halim*, however, is the thick, smooth liquid that is extracted from the grains when they are soaked and cooked in water for a long period. In this translation we have used terms such as 'thick and smooth', 'to become thick and smooth', 'porridge' or 'porridge-like' whenever *halim*-related descriptive terms were used (e.g. '*halim dār*', '*halim vār*', '*halim dādan*', and '*halim endāxtan*'). There is one occasion in which the author recommends using a type of rice which would produce a thick porridge and in this case we translated '*halim dār*' to 'starchy'.

Dough: In this book, the term '*zavāle*' is translated to 'dough ball' regardless of size. The author also sometimes uses '*zavāle*' as a unit of measurement, referring to the amount of dough needed to make one loaf of bread, or the average portion of noodles (i.e. *čāne*).

When the author speaks of '*āš boridan*', he is providing different instructions on how to cut different shapes of noodles, both for noodle soups and noodle pilafs. A full list of the shapes of all the noodles and dumplings used in the manuscript and their description can be found in Table Two.

Two common terms that were used when referring to the texture of the dough are '*dombe xamir*' (literally: tail fat dough) and '*xamir-e mohkam*' (firm dough); these expressions describe the texture that the dough should have. The former, a moist dough with a higher liquid content in relation to the flour weight – and thus soft and sticky, like tail fat – has been translated to 'loose dough', while the latter, a hard, well kneaded, less moist dough, has been translated in this text to 'firm dough'.

Serving: At the end of the recipes, the pot is instructed to be removed from the fire. The term that has often been used for this is '*foru ārand*' (literally: take down). We have translated this phrase in the literal form, but added a bracket as a means of clarification: 'take down [the pot]'.

More often than not, the dish is to be served in a porcelain serving dish (*čini*). As the term '*čini*' has been vaguely used – usually without the indication of the specific type of the serving dish – we decided to translate it to 'china' and hint at the type of serving dish in brackets.

Units of measurement

Before the early twentieth century and the implementation of the metric system in Iran, old units of measurement were mostly used and they are constantly found in this text, too. Although we have replaced the old units by metric units, wherever possible we often include the original units, as standardization would have made the recipe more difficult to read. A full list of the measurements that have been used in this text and their metric equivalents can be found in Table Three.

There are also some 'casual' measurement units to measure size, width, or length, such as 'palm-size', 'finger-size', 'finger-width', 'the size of almond/chickpea/broad bean' and so on. These measurements were generally used to specify cutting certain meats or vegetables. We could find only a couple of metric equivalents for chickpea-size (0.2 gr) and finger-size (4.4 cm) in the 'official' old system of measurement; however, we can never know how exact Bavarchi was in using these casual forms of measurement.

Table One: Equipment

Equipment (in text)	Description	Equivalence (in translation)
Bādie	Large bowl usually made of copper	Large bowl
Čini	Porcelain dish of any shape	China
Dig	A large cooking pot or caldron made of copper	Pot
Dig-e sefid	Literally white pot; a copper pot that is coated with a layer of tin	Tinned [copper] pot
Digče	A small pot	Small pot
Gāz	A kind of tool similar to scissors or pincer	Scissors, tool
Kafče	Ladle or spatula	Ladle
Kafgir	Literally foam remover; skimmer	Skimmer
Karbās	Thin white cotton cloth similar to muslin or cheesecloth	Muslin
Komāj-dān	A copper or earthenware cooking pot with lid similar to Dutch oven	Pan
Qāšoq	Spoon	Spoon
Rismān	String, thread, rope	String
Sāj	Griddle	Griddle-pan
Six	Skewer	Skewer
Som-tarāš	Hoof trimmer, tool used when trimming horses' or cows' hooves	Paring iron
Suzan	Needle	Needle
Šarbati	Bowl, small copper bowl	Bowl
Tanur	Tandoor	Tandoor
Tašt	A wide metal basin, deeper than a tray but shallower than a tub.	Tub
Toršipālā	Metal colander	Colander

Table Two: Noodles

Names	Literal translation	Description
Band-e qabā[4]	Robe's band	Long, wide, flat noodles
Barg-e bid	Willow (tree) leaf	Short flat pieces of noodles
Boqrā		Flat disks of noodle
Jovak	Small barley	Small barley-shaped noodles
Jušpare		Small filled noodles
Leng-e barre	Leg of lamb	Flat, large, fusiform noodles
Mahiče-ye bārik	Thin muscles	Flat, thin (and small) fusiform noodles
Manto		A type of filled noodles
Omāj	Rubbed thing (Turkish)	Small thin noodles, similar to rice grains
Pulāni		Large flat disks with knurled edge
Rešte	String	Long, thin, flat noodles
Sangrize	Pebbles	Small chickpea-sized balls
Sarangošti	Fingertip-shaped, shaped by fingertips	Small disks (perhaps) shaped by fingertips
Totmāj	Sumac soup (Turkish)	Flat squares (or circles) of noodles
Zabāngonješk	Ash (tree) leaf	Long ellipse shaped noodles
Zolf-e yār	Lover's hair	Twined pieces of noodles

4. *Qabā* is a type of sleeved, tailored, midcalf-length coat open down the front and closed by one side being fastened with a band across the other.

Table Three: Units of measurement

Unit (in text)	Equivalence	Equivalence (Metric)
1 *man*	600 *mesqāl*	2784 grams
1 *čārak* (= a quarter)	0.25 *man*	742 grams
1 *sir*	16 *mesqāl*	74.2 grams
1 *mesqāl*		4.64 grams
1 *noxod* (chickpea)		0.2 grams
1 *gaz*		1 metre
1 finger		4.4 cm

Table Four: Romanization

No	Equivalent in Persian Script	Symbol	IPA Equivalent	No	Equivalent in Persian Script	Symbol	IPA Equivalent
1	ؤ - ع - ء	'	[ʔ], Ø	16	ن	n	[n]
2	َـ	a	[æ]	17	ُـ	o	[o]
3	آ - ا	ā	[a:]	18	پ	p	[p]
4	ب	b	[b]	19	غ - ق	q	[ɢ]
5	چ	č	[tʃ]	20	ر	r	[r]
6	د	d	[d]	21	ث - س - ص	s	[s]
7	ِـ	e	[e]	22	ش	š	[ʃ]
8	ف	f	[f]	23	ت - ط	t	[t]
9	گ	g	[g]	24	او - و	u	[u:]
10	ح - ه	h	[h]	25	او	ow aw	[ow] [æw]
11	ی	i	[i]	26	و	v	[v]
12	ج	j	[dʒ]	27	خ	x	[χ]
13	ک	k	[k]	28	ی	y	[j]
14	ل	l	[l]	29	ذ - ز - ض - ظ	z	[z]
15	م	m	[m]	30	ژ	ž	[ʒ]

Cook's Notes: Catheryn Kilgarriff

I cooked the recipes in the photographs, and as an experienced cook, adjusted the quantities for around four people easily. It seems that Bavarchi cooked in large quantities as a *man* is over 2 kilos in weight. I also used filo pastry instead of thin bread for the baklava, and one could use ready-made noodles, rice or wheat, as preferred. The spices were aromatic, and the house was full of the aroma of cinnamon, truly lovely.

The photographer, Nadia Mackenzie, and I bought the spices and props from the shop *Persepolis* in Peckham, run by Sally Butcher who wrote *Persia in Peckham* for Prospect Books. Many thanks for her hospitality during the morning we were in her shop.

The Manual

On Cooking and its Craft

by Bavarchi

*

Preface by Bavarchi

[Praised be God who] adorned palatable foods. [All] praise is [due] to God for His graces. The most palatable words that, if spoken by tongue will resemble the nightingale's song, are the sweet recitations of the name of the sweet-tongued [prophet] who seasoned enthusiasm among the Arab and the non-Arab by his miraculous eloquence, and who sweetened the desire of people of faith by his honey of sacrifice – blessing of God be upon him, his family, and his devotees.

And now, this is a treatise in the craft of cookery, consisting of twenty-four[1] chapters and a postface, on the description of colourful meals and varicoloured foods, composed by the guiding God's humblest servant, *Hāji Mohammad Ali Bāvarči Baqdādi* – may God forgive him and his parents, and may God do good to them and him – as a gift to the most high, noble House of His Majesty *Mirzā'i*, the supereminent, the angel-mannered, the justice-renowned, the bounteous, the famed, the ruler of the people's affairs in the universe, the abrogator of injustice among nations, the stalwart of the conquering Sultanate, the pillar of the shining Caliphate, the refuge of the grandest elite and royal, the fortress of the noble grandee of the parts and tracts [of the world], the paragon of the warrior and the intellectual, the fount of all the nobilities and ethics and virtues, the mentor of the scholar and the discoverer, and the strengthener of the weak and the poor – may God perpetuate the shadow and glory of his fortune upon all beings till the Day of Resurrection.

Let it not remain concealed from the bright, brilliant mind of [every] prosperous nabob – may they receive abundant blessings and the best eternal dwelling – that this humblest [of men] has written what he has acquired in this craft (of cookery) during his lifetime, what he has learnt by seeking guidance from skilled masters, and what he has studied in the books of the wise men, in this brief treatise so the noble and the commoner

1. See the translators' introduction about the discrepancy in the number of chapters.

will benefit from it, and call down blessing on this modest servant.

And this manuscript was compiled during the reign of *Soltān-ebn-e Soltān-ebn-e Soltān Ab-ol Mozaffar Soltān Šāh Esmā'il Bahādor Xān,*[2] the Great King of auspicious fortune, the king-making and world-conquering emperor, the *qibla* of all the sultans in the universe, the paragon of all the renowned khans, the extender of security and safety, and the propagator of justice and kindness – may God the Exalted perpetuate the permanence of his caliphate and his reign.

And the cause of writing this manuscript, which is named *Kārnāme*, was that this humblest [of men] was led, by the aid of God, to *Dār ol-Ershād-e Ardabil* in the year 927, and had the honour of making the pilgrimage to his Holiness the Sultan, the guardian of the state and the king of the realm of guidance, *Soltān Šeix Safi* and *Soltān Šeix Haydar* – may peace be upon them both – and paid respect to chiefs and the sheikhs.

At the time of return, being manifestly aware of the reverence of his most high throne, I did not have a gift that was worthy enough for the House of [he who is] the centre of the universe, the propitious nabob – may his fortune be perpetuated. Suddenly, from the World of the Unseen, it crossed my languished mind to compile a manuscript on Cookery and Its Craft that, heretofore, no one has complied or been in possession of, so it can be presented, as a gesture of benefaction, to the respected dignitaries of the state – may God eternize their fortune – so by this means, the life of this humble servant will be taken notice of, the people will benefit, and [my] fame will be emblazoned.

All have gone sweeping in the garth of lore
And what I tell hath all been told before[3]

In short, what I have seen in the books of the wise men or heard [from them], and what I have learnt from preceding masters and then developed, as well as a few innovations based on the experience that God the Exalted has granted to this humblest [of men] during his lifetime, the account and description of each will be explained fully so that whoever desires whatever colourful meal can, upon reading this book and gathering and concocting

2. Referring to Shah Ismail I, the founder of the Safavid Dynasty, ruling from 1501 to 1524.
3. Poem by Ferdowsi, translation of Arthur George Warner and Edmond Warner.

the ingredients, procure that which is desired to its most perfect state.

There is a great deal [that needs to be explained] in this *Kārnāme*. [However,] I have essayed to be brief to avoid lengthening. From God comes all aid and in Him is [our] trust.

And this treatise contains twenty-six[4] chapters:

Chapter One: recipes for varieties of *komāj* (stuffed breads)

Chapter Two: recipes for *āš-haye ārdine* (noodle stews) and the cutting of each [noodles]

Chapter Three: recipes for *āš-e halim* (porridge), barley *āš* with kid and verjuice

Chapter Four: recipes for *šurbā-ye boqrāti* and *šurbā-ye pirbudāqi* (mixed meat stews) and its likes

Chapter Five: recipe for thin *noxodāb* and thick *noxodāb* (chickpea soups) and its likes

Chapter Six: recipes for *māst-bā, šir-berenj, labaniyye* (dairy soups) and its likes

Chapter Seven: recipes for *āš-e serke* (vinegar stew), *mozavvare-hā* (soups for the sick), sour *āš* and its varieties

Chapter Eight: recipes for wheat and barley *harise* (porridge, harissa), wheat and barley *kaškak*, milk and wheat *harise*, and varieties of *harise-hā* [made of] shelled pistachio and rice

Chapter Nine: recipes for *šile palaw-hā* (sticky rice dishes) which are some kinds

Chapter Ten: recipes for *dāne palaw-hā* (grainy pilafs) which are some kinds

Chapter Eleven: recipes for *qabuli, rešte palaw, jovak palaw* (noodle pilafs) and their likes

Chapter Twelve: recipe for *moza'far palaw* (saffronned pilaf) with hen and *kallemāčān* with *moza'far* (sheep's head and trotters with saffronned pilaf)

Chapter Thirteen: recipes for *siah palaw-e nārdān, palaw-e āb-e limu va nārenj, palaw-e qure va somāq* (sour pilafs) or else

Chapter Fourteen: recipes for *palaw-e zard, palaw-e sorx*, and *palaw-e sabz* (colourful pilafs)

4. Although twenty-six chapters are listed here, the manuscript only contains twenty-two.

Chapter Fifteen: recipes for *sambuse-ye morrasa' va sāde* (jewelled and plain samosa), *qottāb*, and *šakarbure* (stuffed pastries)
Chapter Sixteen: recipe for *beryān-hā* (roasts) which are some kinds
Chapter Seventeen: recipes for *qaliye-hā* (braised meat stews) which are some kinds
Chapter Eighteen: recipe for *motanjane-hā* (fried dishes) which are some kinds
Chapter Nineteen: recipes for *gipā-hā* (stuffed tripe) which are some kinds
Chapter Twenty: recipes for kebabs which are some kinds
Chapter Twenty-One: recipes for *zonnāj* and *šorāyeh* (sausages and fritters) which is also called *kabāb-e šāhi* (king's kebab)
Chapter Twenty-Two: recipe for *sirāb*, mutton *jime*, and *qaliye-ye poti* (offal and tripe dishes)
Chapter Twenty-Three: recipes for *qarmāni* and plain baklavas and *čalpak*
Chapter Twenty-Four: recipes for wild herbs and vegetables and how to cook each
Chapter Twenty-Five: recipes for *halvā-hā* and *pālude, fereni*, and *rešte-ye qatāyef* (sweets, puddings, and pastries)
Chapter Twenty-Six: recipes for jams and how to cook each.

And the description of the making and characteristic of each will be explained in its own chapter so, at the time of cooking, the given recipe can be applied to procure that which is desired.

Chapter One

On Komāj[1] Breads

Bāb-e avval: Dar sefat-e anvā-e komāj-hā

Making Bread - Plain Komāj

Dar sefat-e komāj-e sāde

As bread stands before all food,[2] it shall be spoken of first. Take, say, a *man* of maida flour and one and a half *čāraks* of oil. It would be better to substitute the amount of water used in [making] the dough with the same amount of milk. Soak some yeast in lukewarm water for awhile and rub with [your] hands and [then] squeeze it through clean fine muslin. Put the flour in a clean dish and make the necessary amount of dough, and add ingredients (*havāej*) such as mastic and fennel – whatever is desired – which would improve it. Make a good dough that is loose (*dombe xamir*) and let it be awhile. While the dough is to be done (leavening), prepare an oven, the size of the pan, for the pan and kindle the fire there.

Once the dough is done, grease the pan, make a dough ball, place it in the pan, and stretch the dough with [your] fists to the size of the pan and smear the top with a little yogurt or dissolved saffron in water so that it

1. Or *komāč,* a type of leavened bread that is usually stuffed with sweet or savoury fillings and is baked in a pan similar to Dutch oven and baked in hot ashes.
2. Bread is a culturally significant food in Iran. It must be respected as it symbolizes holy blessings and fortune.

browns while baking and cover the pan. Take the fire that has been burnt out of the stove, replace it with the pan, and put some of that fire ash over the lid of the pan. If the fire is weakening, burn some fire over it. Do not neglect the excess or dearth of fire until it is well cooked.

Making Bread - Quince Komāj

Sefat-e komāj-e beh

Take, say, a *man* of white maida flour, a *čārak* of oil, half a *man* of milk, and water as much as it needs, mastic brittles, and a little yeast, and make a good dough and let it be [awhile] until it is done. Kindle the fire in the place for the pan and make two dough balls: one for the bottom and the other for the top. Prepare four large sweet quinces, and if it is desired, eight large assorted apples. Cut the top of the quinces or apples, whichever there is, one-finger-width-size, and dig out the inner of the quince with a tool such as paring iron so that its skin is not punctured and does not become too thin either. Remove the quince seeds from the flesh and dice the flesh well and add the amount of half a *čārak* of ground peeled almonds, half a *čārak* of ground pistachios, and half a *čārak* of ground white sugar and some musk and rosewater, mix all these together, stuff the quinces, and place the top of the quinces [back] in place.

Devise a nail out of quince stem or any other available wood and secure the top of the quince. Place these quinces in between the two rolled out [balls of] dough. Secure the edge of both dough balls together with the fingertips so that they would not detach and [the edges] stick together. Place the lid of the pan over it [to size the loaf] so it fits well in the pan.

Remove the extra rim and pleat up the edge as you would for *šakarbure*.[3] Once it has been placed in the pan in a way that four quinces are in the four corners, cut squares with a knife in the top dough that is between each two quinces so that while cooking, each [quince in each] corner would become visible. Cover the pan with its lid and take out the fire that was

3. See recipe in Chapter Fourteen.

burnt in the place of the pan, put the pan there, and put the fire, which was taken out, back on top of the pan. If the fire weakens, kindle [more] fire on top, and attend well to the fire so it would not surpass nor weaken. Once it is cooked, at the time of taking out, you must place a tray that is bigger than the top of the pan over the pan and must hold the tray and the pan firmly together. [Then] flip it fast, lest it fall apart. Follow the instructions so it would not be spoiled.

Making Bread - Jewelled Komāj

Dar sefat-e komāj-e morrassa'

Take, say, a *man* of white maida flour and half a *čārak* of mutton tallow, water, and the necessary amount of salt. Make a firm dough and wrap it in wet muslin. Dice a *man* of meat and fry in oil with onion, cumin, and coriander, and if [desired] add sumac juice or lemon juice. Boil it until [its liquid dries up and] oil appears. Make twenty-four dough balls and spread twelve [of these dough balls] thinly on a board and place them in the pan and grease until all the twelve [pieces] are done. Firmly press with the fingertips the edge of the dough (*nān*) to the edge of the pan. Put the fried meat filling (*qeyme*) in, grease the other twelve [pieces of stretched] dough and place them over the meat filling. If [desired], instead of[4] the meat filling grind a *čārak* of ground shelled and peeled almonds with half a *čārak* of white sugar, mix together with some rosewater, and place it in the *komāj* and meat filling.

If it is desired, throw a fistful of ground sugar between each [layer] of the greased dough which would be better. Firmly press the edge of the dough to the edge of the pan with the fingertips and cut off its extra [rim] with a knife. Prepare half a *čārak* of peeled almonds, half a *čārak* of shelled pistachios, a *čārak* of green raisins, half a *mesqāl* of saffron, and six cooked eggs cut in half, all while the bread bakes.

4. *Be avaz-e qeyme.* The author instructs to replace the meat filling with the almond mixture. However, in the next sentence he orders to add the almond mixture to the meat filling.

[Meanwhile, take] a *čārak* of white maida flour, four eggs, and some salt. Crack the four eggs in the flour and saffron and make a batter with some water like the batter[5] for *zolubia*.[6] [Take] half of the batter, heat a *čārak* of oil in a small pot, and take fistfuls of the batter and sprinkle in that oil [and fry] until it sets, and take out quickly. Smear the top of the *komāj* with some of the batter. Sprinkle immediately the shelled almonds, pistachios, and raisins in [some of] that batter [and fry in oil].

Then, mix all the fried [ingredients] in the batter, and [place] over the *komāj*, and even out. Mix the six halved, cooked eggs with some batter and secure them on the other ingredients (*havāej*) [over the bread]. Pour half a *čārak* of warm oil slowly over it and secure the lid of the pan. Set the fire aside, place the pan there [where the fire was burnt], and put the fire on top of it. If it (the fire) weakens, burn some logs over it (the pan) and tend to the fire. Do not neglect the excess or dearth of the fire until it cooks; take the lid off a few times to test [if] it is cooked. At the time of taking out, prepare a tray that is larger than the lid of the pan, fold a few metres (*gaz*) of clean muslin and place it over the bread. Place the tray on the opening of the pan, hold it firmly and flip quickly, again, place a tray the same size as the bread over it and flip it quickly so that the jewelled top comes on top and sprinkle sugar and ground musk over it.

Making Bread - Qabuli Komāj

Sefat-e komāj-e qabuli

Take, say, a *man* of white flour, half a *čārak* of oil, the necessary amount of salt and water, and make dough. Add some mastic and

5. *Bolmāj konand. Bolmāj* is a type of thin soup. Here the author uses this word to emphasize that the batter should be thin. In Persian, the word for both batter and dough is *xamir*.
6. Written *zolibia* in text; *zolubia* is a type of sweet, better known as *jalebi* in some countries, and is made by deep-frying a batter in oil.

prepare a firm dough, and [make] twenty dough balls – half for the bottom [crust] and half for the top. Spread ten [of the dough balls] and place in the pan and for the filling (*qeyme*) use anything that is available. Cook elsewhere one *hasib*[7] filled with fried diced meat (*qeyme*), rice, chickpeas, onions, and spices, and put in surrounding all the ingredients (*masāleh*).

After that, for the filling, [prepare] whatever you can such as fried diced meat (*qeyme*), small meatballs, fried hen pieces (*qaliye*) or lamb stew (*qaliye*), peeled chickpeas, shelled almonds, raisins, shelled pistachios, two halved, cooked eggs or peeled, green, broad beans. Also, [prepare different types] of noodles (*ārdine*) such as thin *māhiče*, thin *rešte*, small *jušpare, zabāngonješk*, and *sarangošti*[8] and fry them all in oil. Coil up the *māhiče* noodles around five fingers[9] so they are shaped like skeins and fry them in oil. Cut the carrots into thin rings (*taneke*) and boil, cut the cabbage into strings and boil in a little water.

Cut the onions into extremely thin rings, clean the spinach, and cook in warm water, and then squeeze its water out firmly so it becomes [dry and dense] like an apple. Next, as for the rice, boil the amount of one and a half *čāraks* in meat broth with a little salt. Once the rice is to be done, drain its [excess] water and add a *čārak* of good mutton tallow to the rice and steam with the lid on. [Then,] divide the rice into four parts: leave one part white; colour a part red using foxtail amaranth and sprinkle with ground sugar; colour the rest with saffron and leave half saffroned yellow, and for the other half, powder a little indigo and mix it so it becomes green. If it is desired to have *siah palaw*,[10] too, pound a little pomegranate seeds and currants with one[11] cornelian cherry and boil, strain, [and mix with] the amount of a *čārak* of rice, some peeled almonds, and some raisins. Do not neglect the excess or dearth of water [and cook the rice until] parboiled,[12] add

7. *Hasibak*; the intestines of yearling lamb which has been stuffed with ingredients, similar to *gipā* or *čarbrude* (Chapter Eighteen).
8. See Chapter Two.
9. Bring the five fingertips of one hand together and coil up the noodle around them.
10. See Chapter Thirteen.
11. i.e. a little amount of.
12. *Dāne begirand*; cook the grains only until they begin to soften and are hard inside.

oil – as much as it needs – and stuff fat intestines [with the parboiled rice] and boil in another pot.

All these must be prepared for putting all around the [other] fillings in the *komāj*. If only one of these is desired, that would work, too, as [preparing] all is much work and not everyone can accomplish this. Once all these ingredients (*masāleh*) are ready together, first, coil up the [stuffed] fat intestine by the rim of the bread inside the pan. [Take] those halved eggs and place [four half cut-side up] alternating with four other pieces – cut-side down – on four other sides.

For the noodles (*ārdine*), [place] the *māhiče* in the middle, having sprinkled a little water over each one of the *rešte*, *zabāngonješk, jušpare,* and *sarangošti,* put them over the eggs. Mix some slivered almonds with ground sugar and sprinkle over the places you would like to fill with coloured rice, then piles of coloured rice must be placed on it. The rest of the ingredients (*masāleh*) that were described must be all fitted next to one another adequately and flatly.

Spread out ten dough balls (*nān*), grease, [and place as the top crust over the filling]. It would be better to sprinkle a fistful of ground sugar, ground almond, and rosewater between each dough (*nān*). Seal the edges of the [top and bottom crust] dough together tightly and cut its extra [rim] so they would not detach at the time of taking out. Cover the lid of the pan, remove the fire that has been burnt in the pan's spot, place the pan there, and put the fire that was removed over [the pan].

If it (the fire) is weak, burn more fire on its top. If it was [hot ashes, the remainder of a] burnt fire, it would be better. Take good care of the fire so it would not surpass nor weakens. Remove the lid of the pan a few times and check [for doneness] until it is cooked. At the time of taking out, you must place a dish that is larger than the lid of the pan on top of the pan, must hold firmly together, flip, and shake the sides [of the pan until the bread loosens] and comes out intact. At the time of cutting, an expert or the person who has cooked it and knows how he has assembled everything shall cut it (the bread). The person who would cut this *komāj*, must first place the knife twice crossing the top of the bread, cut, and [be careful] not to cross the knife over the markings (*yarāq*). [Cut the bread on the marked cross] and run the knife around its sides and the markings so it is divided into four pieces.

Place each of these pieces of bread in a china [dish] so the ingredients (*xordani*) would show. Serve each coloured [fillings] over the pieces of bread that have been served in the china plates – in the order they were placed in the pan. Each china [plate] should be arranged neatly as per this method so it would appear well.

Making Bread - Varaq Komāj

Sefat-e komāj-e varaq va san'at-e ān

Take a *man* of white maida flour, the necessary amount of salt, water, and a little ground mastic and make a firm dough and wrap it in damp muslin for awhile. Fry in oil a *man* of [diced] meat, half a *man* of onions, and whatever spices [are] available. Or make the raw [ingredients] the size of poppy seeds[13] as this filling (*qeyme*) would produce a more pleasing result. Then, make twenty balls out of the dough and flatten them on a board in a way that they would not stick to it (the board). Smear oil on the board, spread each of the dough balls thinly one by one and smear each with the oil of freshly melted pieces of suet, fold [each dough] again, make dough balls [and spread each] larger than the pan. Place ten of the spread dough (*nān*) for the bottom [crust], put the filling (*qeyme*) over it, and place the other ten doughs over the filling (*qeyme*) the same way. Press the edges of the crusts (*nān*) firmly together with the fingertips, put the lid of the pan on it [to size the bread] and cut out the extra rim with a knife and pleat up its edge as [you would for] *šakarbure*,[14] pick it up intact, and place in the pan, kindle the fire underneath as per the [usual] method and take good care of the fire. If it (the fire) weakens, burn more fire on top of it, and pour and the amount of a *čārak* of oil over and under it, secure the lid, and place under the fire.[15] At the time of taking

13. i.e. mince the raw ingredients.
14. See Chapter Fourteen.
15. This can also be translated to 'kindle fire underneath it'.

out, place a dish that is bigger than the pan over the pan, hold them both together tightly, and flip quickly. Again, place another china [dish] that is its size over the bread and flip again so it sits well in the china. At the time of taking out, place some metres (*gaz*) of folded clean muslin over the pan and flip so the bread would not be spoiled. Pound some good white sumac, sift, and sprinkle when it is wanted which would be better and God knows best.

Chapter Two

On Noodles

Bāb-e doyyom:

[Dar sefat-e āš-hāye ārdine va san'at-e boridan-e ān]

Making Noodles - Māhiče Āš

Sefat-e [āš-e] māhiče

Take white maida flour, say, a *man*, and the necessary amount of water and salt. If it is desired, soak some saffron in water and make dough with that saffron water so it would be saffron yellow. Make some dough using foxtail amaranth water [so it would be red]. Make white dough with some [of the plain flour], and knead to flat, thin *māhiče*, make a good dough and punch a lot. At the end, grease it with mutton tallow, punch again, and cover it in damp muslin for awhile, then knead [again] which would be better. [Take] fat meat, as much as is desired, and dice some and pound some (to make meatballs), and cook with onions, warm spices, plenty of peeled chickpeas, saffron, and cinnamon until it becomes quite fall-apart tender, add the necessary amount of water and throw in some spinach, too. It would be better to use meat broth for [cooking] the *māhiče* noodles. There must be much boiling water so the *māhiče* turns out perfectly, and boil them for [a] long [time]. Once it has boiled for some moments, take [the pot] down.

At the time of serving, make the condiments out of vinegar and grape molasses together with garlic and dried mint; or boil vinegar and sugar; or lemon juice and Seville orange [juice] and sugar; or mint water; or pounded, boiled, and strained pomegranate seeds and currants mixed with pounded garlic and [dried] mint. If *kašk* is desired or strained yogurt [mixed] with garlic and [dried] mint, it would work, too. Any of all these condiments can be added to all types of noodle soups (*āš-e ārd*). Serve *māhiče* noodles in a dish, add the condiments, add enough of the meat base (*qeyme*) to each dish, adjust the salt and condiments so nothing is lacking and eat.

Making Noodles - Māhiče Āš II

Dar sefat-e māhičebor va san'at-e ān

Take young fat meat, as much as is desired, and add the necessary amount of water in a pot [and heat. Throw the meat in] and remove the foam. Dice some and pound [some] (to make meatballs). Once the meat and the diced meat (*qeyme*) are done, take maida flour and make a firm dough, punch a lot, and cover in clean damp muslin for awhile. After that, make dough balls the size of big pomegranates and, on a board, spread [each ball] thin but do not spread it too thin, fold, and cut into rectangles with a sharp scissors. Pick up [each of the rectangle shaped pieces] from the board, dust it with flour and with the other hand pull gently and slowly from top to bottom so it is flattened and looks like a muscle and does not break.[1] Throw in the pot of meat broth and cook. At the time of serving, any condiment that was mentioned in the recipe of *māhiče* (the previous recipe) can be used in this, too, which would be good.

1. We imagine that each rectangular piece of dough should be picked up and pulled, while it is held in both hands from two opposite corners, so it resembles the fusiform muscle shape.

On Noodles

Making Noodles - Jewelled Boqrā[2]

Sefat-e boqrā-ye morrassa' va san'at-e ān

Take white maida flour, as much as is wanted, and meat, as much as is wanted, and chop larger than almond-size. Chop some tail fat, too. First, half-fry the tail fat and throw the diced meat in that oil and half-fry it. Throw in a skimmer[full] of ringed onions and sauté it. Having brought [some] water close by the pot, pour the necessary amount of water in the fried meat pieces (*qaliye*), add peeled chickpeas, ringed onions, cinnamon, ginger, ground pepper, cumin, and coriander, and steam with the lid on until it becomes fall-apart tender [and its liquid dries up] and oil reappears. Dice some of the meat and pound some (to form meatballs), [fry the meat, and add] peeled chickpeas and spices and steam with the lid on until [its liquid dries up] and oil reappears.

If broad beans are in season, boil some peeled green broad beans separately. Soak some beans and boil separately. Boil some peeled chickpeas separately. Prepare some peeled, shelled almonds and some raisins, each separately. After that, dissolve some saffron in water with enough salt and make a dough with that maida flour. Make some dough with [red] foxtail amaranth water and the necessary amount of salt. Again, make some dough with saffron, powder some indigo in water and knead into that [saffron yellow] dough and punch until it becomes pistachio green, and make some white dough.

If you want to cut the *boqrā* noodles, make a firm dough, spread it on a board and cut with a *boqrā* cutter, [however,] if you wanted to shape it with [your] hands, make a loose dough. Once the *boqrā* noodles are cooked, take them down, [strain] and sprinkle cold water on them. Drain the excess water and [prepare] condiments from vinegar and grape molasses; or lemon juice and sugar; or mint water and sugar; or strained yogurt with garlic and dried mint. Having prepared all these, serve the *boqrā* noodles on a china [plate] or on a wide dish. Put the *boqrā* in the middle and the meat

2. *Boqrā*, short for '*āš-e boqrā xāni*', was the creation or favourite dish of a king of *Khwarazm* named *Boqrā Xān* (ca. 1000 AD). *Boqrā* noodles appear to be shaped like flat disks and cut with a *Boqrā* cutter.

stew (*qaliye*) on one side, the fried diced meat (*qeyme*) on one side, and the meatballs on one side, green broad beans, boiled beans, boiled peeled chickpeas, shelled almonds, and raisins, each separately. It would also be possible to boil some *jušpare* [dumplings], too, and place them on one side. If watery [*boqrā*] is wanted, add the broth of the diced meat or the meat stew, or the *boqrā* water[3] and add whichever condiment that is wanted, and garnish the top with dried mint mixed with warm oil.

If it was served with a little water, the *boqrā* noodles would remain in the middle and the ingredients (*havāej*) would stand in tall piles. [Serve] the diced meat, meatballs, and the meat stew, too, as usual and pour thick, strained yogurt mixed with dried mint, and pounded garlic in vinegar – some of each – not covering the whole thing. Dissolve some saffron in water and, using the fingertip, put some spots over the yogurt so it would appear good, and this is why it is called jewelled.

Noodles and Lamb - Boqrā II

Dar sefat-e boqrā – no'i digar

Take fat lamb and chop it larger than almond-size. Pour the necessary amount of water in a pot [and heat]. Once the water is heated, throw in the meat and enough salt, and remove the foam. Once the meat is boiled for awhile, throw ringed onions, plenty of peeled chickpeas, cinnamon, ginger, ground pepper, saffron, and whatever [else] is wanted. While it is cooking, add spinach, too, and steam with the lid on. Having prepared the *boqrā* dough [and cut the noodles], and having boiled the water for the *boqrā*, start throwing the *boqrā* in, while the meat stew (*qaliye*) is being cooked. Once the *boqrā* noodles are finished and are cooked, take down, and sprinkle cold water on them and remove the excess water. At the time of serving, condiments [such as] pounded and rubbed pomegranate seeds and currants with pounded garlic and dried mint, or vinegar and grape molasses, or vinegar and sugar, or lemon juice and

3. i.e. the boiling water in which the noodles were cooked.

sugar, or mint water and sugar, or strained yogurt [mixed] with pounded garlic and [dried] mint, whichever is desired, can be used as a condiment, which would be good.

Noodles and Lamb - Khwarazm Boqrā
Sefat-e boqrā-ye xārazmi

Take fat hogget and chop larger than almond-size and pour the necessary amount of water in a pot [and heat]. Once the water is heated, wash the meat thoroughly and add to the pot with enough salt and remove the foam. While the meat is cooking, add onions, whole peeled chickpeas – if [it is desired], any peeled [legumes] that is wanted can be used – and cinnamon, ground ginger, whatever spices that are available, and saffron. Examine thoroughly the water for the amount of *boqrā* noodles you have and adjust the water [accordingly] so there would not be any shortage of water when cooking the *boqrā* noodles which would not be good. Throw the *boqrā* noodles in that water [and heat]. Once the *boqrā* noodles are cooked, prepare the condiments – whichever condiments that were desired – which would be good.

Noodles and Lamb - Boqrābor & Sarangošti
Sefat-e boqrābor va sarangošti

Take maida flour, as much as is desired, and chop young fat meat larger than almond-size and prepare according to the recipe of the soup meat bases (*qaliye*) with spices and saffron. Make dough out of the flour, form a dough ball, spread over the board, and sprinkle extra flour on it, fold, and cut with a *boqrā* cutter. Do the same for the whole dough and throw [to cook] in a meat broth which would be better. If *sarangošti* is wanted, make the dough a little softer, form a dough ball, [spread] and cut into long thin separate strips[4] on the board, and then roll like *māhiče*, and sprinkle flour and cut to the size of chickpeas and shape into *sarangošti* with the fingertips. It would turn out better if it was cooked in meat broth. Prepare the condiments as mentioned for the other *boqrās,* which would be good.

Noodles and Lamb or Hen - Āš-e Rešte

Sefat-e āš-e rešte va san'at-e ān

Take fat hogget or young fat hen. Clean it inside and outside, wash, and stuff the hen with onion, cinnamon, diced meat (*qeyme*) and peeled chickpeas, and sew, and [throw] together some slices of fat meat and pour the necessary amount of water that is wanted in a pot [and heat]. Once the water is heated, wash the meat and hen thoroughly, and throw [in the pot], and remove the foam. Throw in the necessary amount of salt, cinnamon, and peeled chickpeas. If it is wanted, cook separately [some] diced meat and meatballs, with peeled chickpeas, and diced onions and add spices, too. If it is wanted, mix the meat base Alexandrian style (*qeyme-ye eskandarāni*) – that is raw – and let the meat broth boil for some moments. After that, once the hen and meat are cooked, take them out, and add the *rešte* in that water. Dice spinach and fresh coriander and throw in. Once it is boiled for a moment, grind some mastic in cold water, throw in, and take [the pot] down, sprinkle some cold water and throw the hen that has been taken out again in the pot so it warms up. *Āš-e rešte* does not need any condiments, however, if it is desired, lemon juice can be added.

The dough for *rešte* noodles must be the firmest of all doughs, spread its dough ball thin, and cut thin and flat with a sharp thin knife. When picking the strings up, try not to tear them apart, and place them in a dish and cover its top so they would not dry out and thus would not break when [they] are thrown in water and come out well. Adhere to all [that] was described.

4. *Alef alef beborand*: from the shape the letter A looks in Persian alphabet.

Noodles and Lamb or Hen
Jušpare and Zabāngonješk
Sefat-e jušpare va zabāngonješk

These two can be cooked together and they would be pleasant. It would be possible to cook each separately, too. Take the necessary amount of hogget and fat hens, as many as is desired, and stuff the hens according to the recipe that was mentioned. Add the necessary amount of water and salt [in a pot, heat, and once it is heated throw in the hens] and remove the foam. Then, throw in peeled chickpeas, diced onions, and cinnamon. If it is wanted, cook diced meat (*qeyme*), meatballs, chickpeas, and diced onions separately and add at the time of serving. Prepare a firm dough while the meat is being cooked, spread on a board and cut into squares like *totmāj*. Having prepared the filling (*qeyme*) from the meatballs, place some in the *jušpare* [shells, and seal the sides] and cook accordingly. Spread some dough balls [to cut into] *zabāngonješk* and cook. Then, first add the *jušpare* to the pot so they boil for some moments, then, throw in the *zabāngonješk* so they boil together, and throw in some spinach and diced fresh coriander. Once it is boiled for a few moments, take [the pot] down, and grind some mastic in cold water and sprinkle. Cover the pot for awhile so the aroma of mastic is absorbed by the food and becomes delectable. Serve in a dish and add some of the diced meat and meatballs that have been separately cooked. For the condiment of this *āš*, [a mix of] sugar and lemon juice would be pleasant.

Jušpare
Sefat-e jušpare – no'i digar va san'at-e ān

Take fat hogget and dice [into] small [pieces] and dice the onions, too. First, fry the diced meat (*qeyme*) in oil, after that, add the onions, warm spices, and some saffron with enough salt. Once the meat filling (*qeyme*) is done, take white maida flour and make a firm dough, shape [into] a dough ball, and spread it on the board, and cut into three finger-width long squares like large *totmāj*, place that cooked filling (*qeyme*) inside and wrap into *jušpare* dumplings. Also cook the diced meat, meatballs, peeled chickpeas, onions, warm spices, and saffron separately for its topping. Then, pour the necessary amount of water in a pot [and heat]. Once the water is heated, throw in the *jušpare*. If there was meat broth [instead of water], it would be better. Take out using a skimmer and serve on a tray or in a china [dish]. A condiment [that is made of] pounded and rubbed pomegranate seeds and currants with garlic, and [dried] mint would be better; or vinegar and grape molasses; or strained yogurt [mixed] with garlic and mint. Throw some of the cooked diced meat topping (*qeyme*) over it and heat some [dried] mint in oil and pour all over it so it looks colourful.

Dumplings - Manto[5]

Sefat-e manto va san'at-e ān

Know that the wrapping of *manto* looks like pomegranate flower[6] and its filling (*qeyme*) is to be cooked like the filling for *jušpare*: fry in oil with warm spices, onion, and saffron. Take white maida flour, make dough, and spread it thin on a board, fold, and using a tool like *boqrā*-cutter – but four times the size of a *boqrā*-cutter – cut the dough like you would cut *boqrā* and put on top of one another and cover with a cloth so they would not dry up. [Then] pick them one by one, place in the palm, stuff with the filling, bring its edge up and round up its top and try to make it

5. Also known as *manti* or *mantu*; a type of dumpling popular in many regions from Europe to China. In Persian dictionaries, however, it is mentioned that the wrappers are made of smaller pieces of flat tripe that have been filled, making *manto* a smaller version of *gipā* (see Chapter Eighteen), yet here and in today's recipes, *manto* wrappers are made of dough.
6. Similar to a moneybag, wide on the bottom and narrow on top with its top pinched and brought together.

look like a pomegranate flower, and secure its bottom like the bottom of a pomegranate. This [dumpling] cannot be cooked in water as it would fall apart, instead pour some water in a pot with a wide opening, or in a pan, place a wide colander on the top of the pot, boil the water, and place the wrapped *mantos* in the colander and place over the top of the pot, kindle the fire, and cover the lid of the pan or pot.

Burn the fire underneath it until the *manto* wrapping is cooked. For its topping, prepare diced meat (*qeyme*), meatballs, peeled chickpeas, with onions and warm spices that have been fried in oil. Gently, pick up the *mantos* one by one and place evenly in a china [dish] or tray, pour the condiment that was mentioned before over it, and the topping (*qeyme*) over it. Sprinkle some dried mint [fried in] some hot oil over it, and sprinkle [more of] the topping which would be good. If [desired], mix together strained yogurt, pounded garlic, and [dried] mint. First sprinkle the topping over it (*manto*), then drop dollops of yogurt over the *manto*, and put spots of some dissolved saffron in water over the yogurt, for it would appear nice, and arrange in an orderly way.

Stuffed Dumplings - Bāvardi[7]

Sefat-e bāvardi va san'at-e ān

Take the fat mutton and some tail fat and dice well with onions and warm spices and pound together until quite pounded. Then, take some flour and make a dough, and spread it on a board and cut into squares according to the instructions for *jušpare* wrappers, put [some] of the pounded filling inside the wrappers and fold it over and seal the sides firmly together so that the filling (*qeyme*) would not leak. Cook the meat base (*qeyme*) separately like other soup bases and [prepare] whatever condiment that is wanted. It would be better if they were cooked in meat broth, and prepare the meat base and condiments and add to it.

7. Of or from *Bāvard*; a medieval Iranian town in Northern *Xorāsān*.

Noodles and Broth - Omāj,[8] Xāle Bibi, Jovak

Sefat-e omāj va Xāle bibi va jovak va san'at-e ān

Take white maida flour and make a firm dough and rub it firmly against a sieve so *omāj* is passed through. If *jovak* is wanted, a make firm dough, pinch [small pieces] by the fingertips and rub [to shape the pieces] like barley so they become *jovak*. Throw diced meat (*qeyme*), small meatballs, peeled chickpeas, cinnamon, and warm spices into meat broth and make *āš* of *omāj* and *jovak*. If *xāle bibi* is wanted, [prepare it] like *omāj* and *jovak* [but] first throw in some rice, once the rice is done, throw in those [noodles] and it becomes *xāle bibi*.

Noodles and Broth

Totmāj, Band-e Qabā, Barg-e Bid, Leng-e Barre & Sarangošti[9]

Sefat-e totmāj va band-e qabā va barg-e bid va leng-e barre va sarangošti va san'at-e boridan-e har kodām

Cutting each of these types [of noodles] is different, but the meat topping (*qaliye*) and condiments are the same for all. As it would have become lengthy, all are described under one category. Take young fat meat and chop larger than almond-size, chop the necessary amount of tail fat, too. First, fry the tail fat and remove its crackling, then, wash the meat and fry it in that oil. Throw into the necessary amount of water [some] peeled chickpeas, ringed onions, cinnamon, saffron or turmeric – whichever is

8. Or *Umāj*; is said to be made by *Soltān Ahmad Sanjar* of the *Seljuq Empire* (1097-1118). *Omāj* is also a type of sweet *halvā* made by crumble pieces of dough made in North-east of Iran and Azerbaijan.
9. *Leng-e barre* and *sarangošti*, though named in the title here, have been described in the next recipe.

available – with cumin and coriander, and steam with the lid on. Make the necessary amount of dough out of maida flour and spread it on a board. Cutting each [of these noodles] is different. If square *totmāj* is wanted, having the dough (*nān*) wrapped in the *exlaw*,[10] pass the knife from the top to the end and cut [a strip] the size of two finger-width wide and cut again into squares so it becomes *totmāj*. For *barg-e bid*, too, as per this method, keep it wrapped in the *exlaw*, and pass the knife cutting [the dough] from the top of the *exlaw* to the bottom, cut again one-finger-width wide from the top to the end. [After] cutting, pick from the ends and little by little cut the both ends so it resembles a willow tree leaf (*barg-e bid*). For *band-e qabā*, having [the dough] spread thinly and wrapped in the *exlaw*, fold it on the board, like folding [the dough to cut] *rešte* and cut the size of one-finger-width wide and it is called *band-e qabā*. The water must be boiling by the time the noodles are cut, dust off the flour from the noodles, and throw into boiling water so they come out perfectly. Once they have boiled for a moment, take [the noodles] out, sprinkle cold water until they set. Drain the water if there was too much. For the condiment, add vinegar and grape molasses; or pounded pomegranate seeds and currants; or strained yogurt [mixed] with pounded garlic and dry mint – whichever is wanted – and serve in a china [dish] or any dish that is desired. [Serving] the meat topping over it and mint mixed in warm oil over it would appear nice. Preparing all these [dishes] is as per this recipe.

Noodles and Broth

Pulāni, Sang-rize, Zolf-e Yār

Sefat-e pulāni va sang-rize, va zolf-e yār va san'at-e ān

Making each one is different but the meat base (*qeyme*) and condiments for all are the same. Take fat hogget and some tail fat. First, [dice the tail fat and fry and remove its crackling, then] dice the meat and fry in the tail

10. *Exlaw* only appears in this recipe and we are unsure of what sort of equipment it is.

fat oil with onion and pour in the necessary amount of water [and heat]. Throw in small meatballs, plenty of peeled chickpeas and add cinnamon, warm spices, and saffron. Throw in spinach, too, and steam with the lid on. Then, take white maida flour and make dough, and if *pulāni* is wanted to be made, pinch out [pieces] the size of a walnut, and like children, roll them into balls in the palm of your hand and again flatten in the palm so it becomes as large as the palm, then using two fingertips knurl its edge. This is called *pulāni*. Then, make strands of that dough and rub them between two hands like *māhiče* noodles and with the fingertips, entwine three times[II] and shape into wisps, and this is called *zolf-e yār*. Also, roll some of that dough and shape into *leng-e barre* and into rolls of *sarangošti*, sprinkle a little flour and cut into a chickpea shape, rub with the palms a few times so they become round and this is called *sang-rize*.

Once the *sang-rize* is [ready] to be thrown in the pot, first, throw in the pot some soaked, whole chickpeas – the same amount as the *sang-rize* – so it boils for some moments. Then, throw in the *sang-rize* so they cook together. For all these types of *āš*, the dough is similar, but the cutting [of noodles] and the making of each pot are of different kinds. *Leng-e barre* can be made out of this dough [which looks] like large *māhiče*. *Sarangošti*, too, must be rubbed and bundled like *leng-e barre*, and must be cut with a knife into chickpea shapes, and shaped with the fingertips on a board. Each could have been explained separately, however, as it would have become lengthy, they were written this way [under one category], for the condiment for all is one type and the meat base is one type. Their meat base, like other meat bases, is fried. The condiments, for all, can be whatever that is desired, poured over the *āš* with garlic and dried mint in warm oil, which would appear good. If there was time, other inventions will be written down, and God knows best.

II. The literal translation: form into '*lām-alef*' (a shape of writing letters L and A in Persian scripts in which the letters are twined looking like an inverted awareness ribbon) with the fingertips and [repeat] like this: la, la, la (three times)..

Chapter Three

On Wheat & Barley Stews

[Bāb-e seyyom: Dar sefat-e āš-e halim va āš-e jo]

Wheat or Barley Āš

Dar sefat-e āš-e gandom va āš-e jo va san'at-e ān

Take clean white wheat and pound well until it turns green.[1] Pour the necessary amount of water in a pot [and place the pot over the fire] until it is heated. Wash fat mutton thoroughly and throw in the pot, remove the foam, and [take] the amount of one *man* of that pounded wheat – if more is wanted [measure] as per this recipe – wash [the wheat] thoroughly a few times, boil in [another] pot so its murky water would be removed by [boiling in] that water, [then] take out of that water and throw over the meat and boil well, stirring with a ladle so it would not stick to the bottom of the pot. If there was too much wheat, remove some with a skimmer. Throw in large [whole] or peeled chickpeas, whichever is desired, cinnamon and dill, and stir with a ladle until the porridge and meat are done. Do not neglect to stir deeply, add the necessary amount of salt, and steam with the lid on. Douse the fire so it stops boiling and add

1. *Čonān ke sabz šavad.*

clarified oil. It would be better to grind a little mastic in cold water and add.

Mutton Stew - Halim Āš

Sefat-e āš-e halim - no'i digar

Take mutton, as much of it as is desired, and [pour] the necessary amount of water [in a pot and heat] and remove the foam. Wash pounded, good, white wheat thoroughly a few times with warm and cold water, and pound it in a mortar until soft, [then] rub it in cold water so the extract is separated from the kernel. Throw all the wheat extract and half of the wheat [kernels] over the meat and stir with a ladle until the meat is half-cooked. Then, throw in diced onions, cinnamon stick, peeled chickpeas, small meatballs, and enough salt and adjust the fire accordingly, lest the fire be doused before its [liquid dries up and] oil appears. Grind some mastic in cold water and throw in and steam with the lid on. If it is desired, spinach and carrots can be thrown in, too.

Barley Stew - Barley Āš

Sefat-e āš-e jo va san'at-e ān

Take white barley and pound well until it turns green, and [take] onions and the necessary amount of fat yearling lamb. [Pour] enough water [in a pot and heat]. Once the water is heated, throw in the meat and remove the foam. Wash the necessary amount of barley four times with warm and cold water so that no barley [husk] remains in its kernels. Pound again, dissolve it in cold water and throw in after the meat. If there was wheat or barley, throw them in the meat broth. Unripe grape [stew] is, for example, the same in that it becomes white because unripe grapes are thrown in after the meat. However, if the wheat or barley is thrown in the pot before the meat, its broth will of course become dark or murky, and this has been experienced. Therefore, it is done this way so it (the broth) becomes white (and clear) and good. Having the extract and the barley thrown over the meat, boil until it all become thick and smooth. Or strain the barley completely through muslin and (press) it through with the back of a ladle so that all the sticky extract (*halim*) escapes the barley kernels [and throw the strained liquid in the pot]. If it is wanted, throw in some barley kernels for its texture, and throw in an ample [amount of] peeled chickpeas, diced onions, and cinnamon. Once it is to be done, throw in spinach and fresh coriander, if plain [*āš*] is wanted. If it is wanted with kid (young goat meat), do accordingly and add verjuice, or lemon juice, or tamarind [juice]. In the summer it would be good with kid, and with goat meat, too. Either [one] that is desired can be cooked, and any of the sour condiments can be added, and sugar to flavour would be good. All [of the steps] must be performed orderly as instructed for the work to be done perfectly.

Vegan Barley Āš

Sefat-e āš-e jo-e sāde-ye bi gušt va san'at-e ān

Take pounded white barley and wash six times with cold and warm water until no husk and debris remain in it, add it to a stone pot, and boil until it releases its thick and smooth extract. Strain it through clean thin muslin and press it through with the back of a ladle so that the smooth and sticky liquid (*la'āb*) escapes the kernels completely and add it to the pot again. Throw in enough salt, spinach, and fresh coriander. Pound peeled shelled almonds in a mortar and dissolve in a little cold water, and strain through clean, thin cotton. Mix a little of that *āš* in the juice (almond milk) to moderate them (their temperature), and throw in the *āš* to cook and [it] becomes white and thick and smooth.

Chapter Four

On Savoury Rice Stews (Šurbā)

Bāb-e chahārom: Dar sefat-e šurbā-ye sāde va mānand-e ān

Chicken and Rice - Bagrationi[1] Šurbā

Sefat-e šurbā-ye boqrāti

Take[2] seven young fat hens, clean and wash with cold water until they are whitened (cleaned). Carve out with the tip of a knife the stomach, crop, wing tips, and the tail end and all the entrails such as lung and liver. There should be no negligence in [cleaning] it. Sprinkle three *mesqāls* of pounded, soft, white salt [over the hens] and let them be awhile. Pour the necessary amount of water in a silver pot [and heat], wash thoroughly those hens with cold water so the excess salt is removed from them and throw in the pot. Boil two good cinnamon sticks, three whole, white onions, and a fistful of unpeeled, whole chickpeas so they all become fall-apart tender together.

Take the hens out of the pot, select a good chicken and leave it whole, and pound the other six hens in a silver mortar completely until soft. Pour [some] of the water in which the hens were boiled over them (the

1. Perhaps refers to the *Bagrationi* dynasty of Georgia, indicating the recipe's origins.
2. Written 'throw' in the text.

pounded hens), rub, and squeeze through clean, thin cotton. Throw them (the hens) again in the mortar and pound, add [some] of the broth and squeeze [through cotton]. Strain the rest of the broth over it so that there will be a large bowl of broth [and boil in the pot]. Open [the lid of] the pot on the stove and throw in the [whole] hen.

Throw in three *mesqāls* of rice and heat gently and slowly over the fire, so its liquid would not dry up until the rice is cooked. Once the rice is done, throw in the amount of five leaves[3] of spinach and five leaves of diced, fresh coriander and steam with the lid on. At the time of taking down, grind some mastic[4] in cold water and add [to the pot], and leave it on the ground for awhile so the aroma of mastic remains in it. At the time of serving, first put the [whole] hen in a large bowl and serve the *āš* over that so it would be good.

The father of this *faqir* had been cooking these soups (*āš*) for the late prince *Mirzā Budāq* [whom] God enlightened his reason. This *faqir* has learnt this [recipe] from his father.

Chicken Breast and Rice - Hen Šurbā

Sefat-e šurbā-ye morq - no'i digar

Take cleaned, meaty, fattened hen and wash with cold water until it is whitened (cleaned). Cut its stomach open and carve out the crop, wing tips, lungs and liver from its inside, wash thoroughly again, and cut into pieces. In a mortar, pound the meat of the hen's breast and [some] of the hen fat with diced onions and warm spices. At the time of throwing in the rice, pour the necessary amount of water in a pot with some salt [and heat]. Once the water is heated, throw the hen meat in the pot and remove the foam. Throw in a *mesqāl* of cinnamon, a fistful of peeled chickpeas, a

3. Not a literal amount, referring to a small amount of spinach and coriander.
4. Written 'cinnamon' in text which appears to be an error as 'mastic' is mentioned in the next sentence. Pounding mastic in cold water is a regular instruction appearing at the end of many recipes.

fistful of diced onions, and two mutton meatballs to enrich the soup (*āš*) so they cook together. After the hen is done, take out the mutton meatballs. Pound the necessary amount of white rice with salt, wash thoroughly, and throw in the pot. If you want it thick and smooth, wash a little of that rice and pound in a mortar, add a little cold water, and strain through a cotton cloth and add to the pot, and stir gently until it becomes thick and smooth. At the time of throwing in the rice, throw in some small meatballs. Once the rice is done, throw in a little spinach and diced, fresh coriander. Pound some mastic in cold water at the time of taking [the pot] down and add. [Then] take down and let it be on the ground for awhile so that the aroma of mastic would remain in it. Serve in a china [dish] for it would be good.

Savoury Lamb and Rice - Lamb Šurbā

Sefat-e šurbā-ye gust-e barre

Take fat lamb, salt, [and let it be] awhile; [cut some pieces] and pound enough of the lamb with tail fat and onions (to make meatballs). Take[5] some pieces of fat mutton, too. Pour the necessary amount of water in a pot [and heat]. Once the water is heated, wash the lamb and mutton thoroughly and add to the pot, remove the foam, and throw in cinnamon, diced onions, and peeled chickpeas. Once the lamb is done, take out. It would be better to take out the lamb and mutton after removing the foam, wash them thoroughly with lukewarm water, strain its broth (*šurbā*), [then] add them to the pot again, and after that, throw in chickpeas and onions. Then, take out once the lamb is done and throw in enough rice. [Throw in] small meatballs, chop some of the meat of the leg of lamb Alexandrian-style (*qeyme-ye eskandarāni*) and throw in the *šurbā*, for it would be better. Once it is cooked, throw in spinach and fresh coriander. Add parsnip (*zardak*) and capers

5. Written 'add' in the text.

if desired. Once the soup (*āš*) is done, grind mastic brittles in cold water and sprinkle and steam with the lid on, for it would be good.

Chapter Five

On Chickpea Soups

Bāb-e panjom: Dar sefat-e noxodāb-e raqiq va qaliz

Thin Chickpea Soup

Sefat-e noxodāb-e raqiq

Take some fattened young hens and hogget. Chop the meat of loin, back, or breast[1] palm-sized and stuff the hens with cinnamon and onion. Pour the necessary amount of water in a pot [and heat]. Once the water is heated, wash the hogget and hens thoroughly and add to the pot, remove the foam with enough salt. [Then] throw in, say, for two hens and a *man* of meat, half a *man* of cleaned whole chickpeas. Throw in cinnamon and diced onions [and cook] until they become fall-apart tender and add some saffron too. When the meat is cooked, throw in some spinach and steam with the lid on for awhile and [then] serve in a dish.

Thick Chickpea Soup

Sefat-e noxodāb-e qaliz va san'at-e ān

Take fattened hens, as many as wanted, and the necessary amount of meat.

1. i.e. loin (including rack), flap, and breast in common English terms for lamb cuts.

Cut the hen's stomach open and take out [its giblets]. Remove the crop, wing tips, and back of its tail, wash thoroughly with cold water so the hen is whitened (cleaned). [Take] cinnamon, diced onion, and some diced meat (*qeyme*) and wash some rice thoroughly, too, and stuff the hen's stomach [with them] and sew. Add to a pot the washed meat, [stuffed] hens, and the necessary amount of water [and heat] and remove the foam. Chop [some meat] palm-sized and stuff two fat intestines with diced meat, peeled chickpeas, enough rice, and warm spices. Having removed the foam off the meat, [add] whitened or peeled chickpeas. For instance, for two hens and a *man* of meat, there must be half a *man* of peeled chickpeas. Apply this rule to all [variations of this recipe]. Having washed the chickpeas thoroughly, throw in, and remove the chickpea foam, too. Throw in diced or ringed onions, cinnamon, and some chickpea flour if you want it thick and smooth. When the meat is done, throw in some small meatballs, too. Throw in some saffron and warm spices with some spinach and steam with the lid on. At [the time of] taking down, grind mastic in rosewater and throw [in the pot, and then] take down for it would be better.

Lamb Chickpea Soup

Sefat-e noxodāb-e gušt-e barre

Take fat lamb and cut to pieces. Pour the necessary amount of water in a pot [and heat]. Once the water is heated, wash the meat thoroughly and throw [in the pot] and remove the foam. Wash thoroughly crushed or peeled chickpeas – whichever there is – and throw in the pot. Add diced onions, cinnamon, ginger, and pepper and throw small meatballs. When the meat is done, throw spinach and steam with the lid on. Grind mastic in cold water and throw in, for it would be good.

Chapter Six

On Dairy Soups

Bāb-e šešom: Dar sefat-e māstvā va širberenj va labaniyye va širpalaw

Yogurt Stew

Dar sefat-e māst-vā[1]

Take lamb or mutton. Pour the necessary amount of water in a pot [and heat]. Throw in the meat and remove the foam. Throw in [rice,] onions, peeled chickpeas, beet,[2] and the necessary amount of salt. Once the rice is half-done, smoothly dissolve good strained yogurt with water and pass it through clean thin muslin and throw it in the pot. Once the yogurt is boiled, cut some spinach leaves in half and throw in with some diced, fresh mint and stripped tarragon leaves. Stir gently with the tip of a ladle until it is cooked. Throw in it ground dried mint and pounded garlic dissolved in cold water, then take down.

Try not to overcook the lamb before the stew (*āš*) is cooked, and if it is already cooked, take it out immediately, and reheat it [later on]

1. *Vā or bā*: Persian term for a type of thick soup or stew.
2. *Selq* (Arabic) in Persian can mean beetroot, beet greens, or chard. As the recipe asks for it to be added at an early stage, and before the other greens, it is more likely that it refers to the root of the vegetable.

within the *āš* when the *āš* is to be done, and [then] serve in a dish which would be nice.

Yogurt Stew II

Sefat-e māst bā – no'i digar

Take yogurt and smoothen it [with water] – or use *duq*[3] – whichever is desired, and strain it through clean muslin. Pour enough water in a pot [and add *duq* or diluted yogurt] and stir with a ladle. When it boils, wash the lamb and throw in it. Throw in some salt, peeled chickpeas, and diced onions. Once the lamb is half-done, throw in the necessary amount of rice and throw in any vegetables that can be attained, such as beet (or beet greens), tarragon, and spinach, mint, or oregano – whichever is available – so they cook together. Dissolve pounded garlic in cold water, too, and fry dried mint in oil to enhance its colour, [then] serve which would be good.

Lamb and Yogurt Stew - Labaniyye[4]

Sefat-e labaniyye va san'at-e ān

Take fat lamb or fat yearling lamb, whichever is wanted and chop palm-sized. Pour the necessary amount of water in a pot [and heat]. Once the water is heated, throw in the meat and remove the foam. [Then] take the meat out of the pot again and wash with lukewarm water, and throw in the pot again so no foam would remain stuck to its flesh. It would [always] be better to remove the foam of any [type

3. *Duq* is a savoury yogurt-based drink, common to drink in the Middle Eastern countries. It is simply made from mixing yogurt with water and some salt. As a traditional term, *duq* also refers to buttermilk; the liquid that is left over from churning butter from milk.
4. From *laban* (Arabic) = milk.

Yogurt Stew II

of] meat that has been thrown in a pot, wash it with lukewarm water after removing the foam, and add it to the pot again. However, it is not heeded advice.

Then, add the *labaniyye*'s meat in the pot. Throw in plenty of peeled chickpeas, diced onions, and cinnamon. Once the meat is done, [take] a *man* of rice, smoothen a *man* of strained yogurt with some water and strain through clean thin muslin. For each *man* of rice, there must be one and a half *mans* of water in the pot. First, throw in the rice, [then] throw in the small meatballs as well. Once the rice is half-done, throw in that strained yogurt. For each *man* of rice, there must be one and a half *čāraks* of oil. Then add the oil together with the yogurt to the pot at the same time, and stir gently and slowly until the rice is done. Throw in some pounded garlic, too. If whole garlic (cloves) are desired, throw in some along with the rice. At the time of taking down, pour over it some sieved, ground, dried mint [mixed] in half a *čārak* of warmed oil, and serve in a dish which would be good. If it was served in a china [dish], pour fried mint poured over the china for it would appear better.

Rice Pudding

Dar sefat-e širberenj va san'at-e ān

Take two *mans* of sheep's milk and mix with half a *man* of water [in a pot] and place over the fire and stir gently and slowly with a ladle until it boils. Then, wash half a *man* of white rice thoroughly and throw it in. Stir gently and slowly with a ladle lest they be curdled until the rice is cooked, and then take down. [Take] the amount of one *čārak* of pitted, excellent dates and stuff each with one shelled almond and one shelled pistachio. Place one by one in a wide tray or a china [dish]. Pour enough of the rice pudding on top of it to fill up the china [dish] and sprinkle ground sugar over it which would be good. Let it be awhile to cool down, and then eat.

Rice Pudding

Milk & Noodle Pudding

Sefat-e šir-o-rešte va san'at-e ān

Take white maida flour and make a firm dough with enough salt and water and cut into thin strings (*rešte*). Take milk, as much as is desired, and for each *man* of milk, add a *čārak* of water and some salt [and heat]. Once the milk is boiled, throw in the *rešte* (noodles) and, if it is desired, throw in some sugar, too. Once it is cooked, take [the pot] down, add a little cold water, and serve in a china [dish]. Having served it in a china [dish], sprinkle ground sugar afterwards for it would be better.

Milk Pilaf

Sefat-e šir palaw

Take half a *man* of rice and two and a half *mans* of milk. If more than this (amount) is desired, [measure] as per this recipe. Then, strain the milk through clean muslin and add to a pot [and heat]. Once the milk is boiled, throw in the rice. It would be better if you pound the rice with salt once more, remove its grits, and wash it with warm and cold water. Having measured the rice and the milk, add for each *man* of rice, a *čārak* of oil and steam with the lid on. [Once it is done] take down and serve in a dish for it would be good.

Chapter Seven

On Sour Stews

Bāb-e haftom: Dar sefat-e āš-e serke va āš-hāye torš

Sour Stew - Vinegar Āš

San'at-e āš-e serke

Take three *mans* of fat hogget; pound one *man* with onion and warm spices and (form into meatballs), and chop two *mans* palm-sized. Pour the amount of two *mans* of water in a pot [and heat]. Once the water is heated, throw in the [chopped] meat and enough salt and remove the foam. Once the meat is boiled for some moments, take it out, and fry in some sesame oil or mutton tallow, add it to the pot again, and throw in the amount of half a *man* of diced onions and a *man* of peeled chickpeas. Soak the amount of one *čārak* of starch in it awhile and mix some water as well, [then] strain it through muslin and add [to the pot]. Boil the amount of one *čārak* of peeled almonds, half a *man* of raisins, a *čārak* of figs, and half a *čārak* of jujubes in water, [then] fry them in oil and throw [the boiled and fried fruits] in it (the pot). Add some ground dried mint and pounded garlic. Having removed the foam of the meat, throw in the big meatballs.

After that, it would be better to throw in the ingredients (*havāej*) and steam with the lid on. At the time of serving, first put some pieces of meat in a china [dish], some meatballs after that, and top with [the rest of] the stew's ingredients, which would be good.

Sumac Flavoured Stew - Sumac Āš

Dar sefat-e āš-e somāq va san'at-e ān

In the profession of cookery there is nothing more difficult than cooking the sumac [stew]. Take perfect large white sumac that has not been dampened, the amount of half a *man* and a *čārak* of white maida flour: rub half a *čārak* with the sumac together, pour the amount of one and half *mans* of water, and let it be awhile. Put [the mixture] in a muslin bag and hang from somewhere. Put a bowl under it so it strains in there. Take the remaining half a *čārak* of flour, take some of that [strained sumac] juice, dissolve [together], and add to that bowl of sumac [juice] again and let it settle thoroughly.

Once the sumac is soaked and strained, you must take three *mans* of fat mutton: pound a *man* with warm spices, salt, diced onions, and a little half-pounded soaked rice. Mix all together and prepare [the meatball mixture] and some peeled cooked eggs. Make two meatballs out of that one *man* of pounded meat [mixed with the spices and rice] and stuff each of the meatballs with an egg. Put each inside a metre (*gaz*) of clean thin cotton, bring its four corners up, and tie its neck with a string, and throw with some salt in another pot so they cook. While the meatballs are being done, cut the meat into four pieces. Pour the amount of three *mans* of water in [another] pot [and heat]. Once the water is heated, wash the meat with water thoroughly two times so any [remaining] blood is removed from its flesh completely and it becomes white (clean) and add to the pot with enough salt [and heat], and remove the foam thoroughly. [Then] take it out of the pot again and make that hot broth lukewarm with a little cold water. Wash off the foam that is stuck to the meat of it, strain the broth through white cotton, too, and wash its pot thoroughly again, too. Pour the broth in the pot, throw in the meat, and kindle a fire [under the pot and heat], and remove the foam as it forms again. Dice the amount of half a *man* of white onions, wash thoroughly, and squeeze through muslin.

Wash half a *man* of peeled chickpeas and throw over the meat. Remove the crown of a white beet off its top, cut into wedges and chop into short [pieces].[1] Scrape the (summer) squash skin and chop into large-finger-sized pieces. Peel the aubergine and prick holes [in it] with a knife, or cut into four pieces, and put in salted water for awhile. Have the rice pounded with ground salt and cook until it is well-whitened. Have a *čārak* of safflower[2] [pounded] and cleaned with water in a mortar, and washed thoroughly a few times so the yellowness is removed from its body. Wash the mortar thoroughly, and pound [the safflower] as you would pound peeled almonds, dissolve in cold water, extract its juice, and let it settle. There will appear on top of it a yellow water (the lees) which will be explained at the end what to do [with it]. Prepare all these ingredients (*masāleh*) before the meat and meatballs are cooked. [Take] that strained sumac, pound a *čārak* of chickpeas, and throw some cold water, rub, and strain through cotton and add to a small tin pot. Pour that strained sumac [juice] through a sieve over the chickpea juice in a way that the sediments that have settled at the bottom would not pass through into it (the small tin pot). Crack two eggs, [separate the yolks] and mix their whites in some water, pour over it, and stir a few times with a ladle so they are mixed together well. Quickly place [the pot] over the fire and blaze the fire so that foam forms on top, and once it is formed, remove that foam and add the sumac[3] over the meat. It would be better to throw some dried bitter orange rinds or lemon rinds after the sumac, to wash the vegetables thoroughly a few times, too, and boil them for a moment in hot water and wash them again with cold water, and add them [to the pot]. It would be better to wash the rice with warm and cold water to whiten it.

Carry out all these [tasks] orderly: first [add] the foam-free sumac [juice] over the meat, then the vegetables, and the rice after that. Once it is time for the rice to be done, take out two shovels of fire (lit charcoals) from the

1. As *selq* could also refer to chard, here, the author might have used silver beets. i.e. separate the leaves of the silver beet, remove the white stem from its back, and chop the green leaves to short pieces.
2. *Qortom* (in Persian from Arabic) or *kāčire*; *Carthamus tinctorius*; a plant that its seeds are used for making vegetable oil and its flower are used as food and textile colouring.
3. Perhaps the sediments.

oven and place the pot on it so it comes to a boil on its own. Once the rice is done, insert a tin ladle inside the pot and stir gently and slowly until the rice becomes sticky. Rub some diced celery with warm water, squeeze [the water out], and throw over the stew. Pour the yellow juice of that extracted safflower [in a bowl], and mix a ladleful of the stew's broth with it and instantly add it to the stew. Pound good white sugar and flavour [the stew] with it. The sourness [of the stew] must be sour enough so the sour taste would not be reduced [much] once it is flavoured with sugar. Pound some garlic until soft, dissolve in water, pour [in the stew], and cover for awhile so it absorbs the garlic aroma. [Then,] take out the large meatballs and remove them from the cotton [in which they were cooked]. Pour a ladleful of their broth in a dish and wash their scum (with that broth), and place them gently in the pot.

The meatballs are added to the pot last as they are large, so that they would not fall apart unexpectedly. At the time of serving, first place the pieces of meat in a large china bowl (*bādiye*) and [then] a meatball, a few aubergines, and the necessary amount of *āš* which would be good, and be attentive and precise.

Chicken or Lamb Tamarind - Tamarind Āš

Sefat-e āš-e tamr-e hendi

Take fat hogget or fattened hen or fat lamb. If [desired, use] the hen and hogget together, if not each singly. The meat must be chopped larger than palm-sized and some of the hogget must be pounded, too, with onions, spices, and enough salt (to make meatballs). Soak the tamarind in water. Then, [boil] the meat with some water and remove the foam. Strain the [soaked] tamarind and pour into it. If it (the tamarind) was not soaked, boil, strain, and pour it over the meat. It is also possible to boil and strain [the tamarind, then] wash the meat and throw in it (the pot of tamarind) [to cook together]. After that, [add] diced onions, peeled chickpeas, shelled almonds, raisins, the necessary amount of rice, and diced fresh mint. Once the rice is done, flavour with sugar, and throw in dried mint for it would be good.

Chicken Tamarind (Tamarind *Āš*)

Sumac Stew - Sumac Āš II

Sefat-e āš-e somāq – no'i digar

Take half a *man* of good white sumac and a *čārak* of good white flour. Rub the sumac and flour together. Pour the entire amount of water (that is needed) for the desired amount of stew over the sumac, stir the water and sumac [mixture] with a ladle a few times, let it soak, and [then] strain. Then, pour the strained sumac [juice] in a pot. Pound some chickpeas, dissolve in cold water and squeeze [through muslin] in the sumac [juice]. Dissolve two egg whites in cold water and pour in the sumac [juice] and stir all together with a ladle a few times and place it over the fire. Blaze the fire and remove the foam. [Take] three *mans* of fat meat, chop some palm-sized and pound some to make meatballs. Having removed the foam off the sumac [mixture], wash the meat thoroughly and throw in the pot and remove the foam of the meat, too. Add some diced onions and crushed peeled chickpeas. Chop beet, peeled aubergines, and squash, wash, and throw in. Throw in the egg-sized meatballs and throw in less rice. Wash peeled almonds and cleaned green raisins thoroughly and throw in. When the rice is not yet done, dice celery and throw in, and when the rice is thoroughly cooked, pound garlic and dissolve in cold water and throw in, remove [the pot from the heat], and serve in a dish.

Bitter Orange, Lemon, and Mint Water Āš

Sefat-e āš-e nārenj va limu va araq-e na'nā

They are all alike in their preparation. Take the necessary amount of fat mutton or fattened hen and cut into slices. Pour the necessary amount of water in a pot [and heat]. Once the water is heated, throw in the meat, remove the foam, and add diced onions and peeled chickpeas. Having removed the foam and thrown in ingredients (*masāleh*), add lemon juice or bitter orange juice, whichever there is. Remove the foam and throw in the necessary amount of chopped beet and fresh mint. After that, throw in rice, shelled almonds, and raisins and when the time of throwing in the rice comes,[4] throw in dried mint and flavour with sugar which would be good.

Pomegranate Seed Āš

Sefat-e āš-e nārdān

Take fat mutton, say, three *mans*; slice two *mans* and pound a *man* (to make meatballs). Take half a *man* of good juicy pomegranate seeds and half a *man* of *Šāhāni* currants[5] and pound together, pour the necessary amount of water and rub with the palms, and strain through a colander. Pour water [over the pounded fruits] again and strain [into a pot], then, place over the fire and boil. After that, wash the meat thoroughly and throw it in. Throw in diced onions, the necessary amount of peeled chickpeas, and egg-sized meatballs. Throw in rice, the necessary amount of shelled almonds, raisins, and strip cut beetroot[6] earlier so they are cooked. After the rice, throw in some dried apricot, too. Once the rice and meat are done, at the time of taking [the pot] down, throw in pounded garlic dissolved in cold water and dried mint for it would be good.

Pomegranate Āš

Sefat-e āš-e anār

Take fat mutton or fat lamb, whichever is wanted, slice [some] and pound some, too. Pour the necessary amount of water in a pot and heat. Once the water is heated, throw in the meat and remove the foam. Throw in the

4. Comparing to the other similar recipes in this manuscript, the instructions should have been: once the rice is done, throw the dried mint etc.
5. Currants made from *Šāhāni* grapes, also known as *šāni*. Usually used for wine making.
6. i.e. beetroots that have been cut to strings; julienned beetroots.

necessary amount of salt, peeled chickpeas, and diced onions. Squeeze the juice of fresh pomegranates and add.[7] Throw in the rice once the meat is done. Once the stew is done, throw in pounded garlic and ground dried mint, steam with the lid on for awhile so the aroma of the garlic is absorbed by it and becomes delectable.

Fresh Fruit Āš

Sefat-e āš-e qure-ye tāze va āluče va zardālu-ye tāze va ālu-ye tāze va san'at-e ān

You must boil and strain [all] for it (the stew) to be good. Take fat hogget or fat lamb and slice them and pound some (to make meatballs). Pour the necessary amount of water in a pot [and heat]. Once it is heated, throw in the meat and remove the foam. De-stem the unripe grapes and throw over the meat with enough salt and some stale or fresh bread and boil together. Once the unripe grapes are cooked, take the pot down immediately. Take the meat out and wash thoroughly so the unripe grape pomace would not remain in the meat flesh. Strain the unripe grape, wash the pot thoroughly, and add the [strained] unripe grape and broth again in the pot, kindle the fire and [add] diced onions, peeled chickpeas, chopped beet, [chopped] celery, and if there was also squash [to add] it would be better. Throw in all and throw in the meatballs, too. Once it is the time for the meat to be cooked, throw in enough rice so they are done together. At the time of taking [the pot] down, throw in pounded garlic and ground dried mint. [For] cherry plum stew, apricot stew, and damson plum stew, boil these all and strain [their juice]. If [desired] throw the meat in another [pot of] water, [heat,] and remove the foam and throw in whichever of the strained juices, the ingredients (*masāleh*), meatballs, and rice. Or else, pour any of the strained juices there is in a pot, adjust the water, wash the meat and throw in, [heat,] and remove the foam, and throw in the vegetables, ingredients, meatballs, and rice together. Once it is cooked, throw in garlic and mint [for] it to be good.

7. The next page starts with 'throw' which seems to be redundant.

Rhubarb Āš

Sefat-e āš-e revāj[8] va san'at-e poxtan-e ān

Take fat mutton or fat lamb and cut into pieces. Pour the necessary amount of water in a pot [and heat]. Wash the meat thoroughly, throw [in the pot], and remove the foam. Then take fresh rhubarb, peel it, and chop into one-finger-sized [pieces] and pound. After that, pour some ladlefuls of the broth in it and rub with the palm so it (the rhubarb) releases its sour taste and squeeze it through clean muslin well so that its juice releases. Wash the meat and pot thoroughly, pour the sour [juice] in the pot, throw in the meat, and kindle the fire and remove the second foam again. Throw in diced onions, peeled chickpeas and beet. Throw in the large, egg-sized meatballs. After that throw in the rice and throw in celery and diced fresh mint. Once the meat and rice are done and are ready, throw in pounded garlic and ground dried mint at the time of taking [the pot] down. It would be better if it was flavoured with sugar. Apple and rhubarb stews are alike. It is also possible to add the rhubarb or apple in a pot, boil, and strain, and having removed the foam of the meat, throw in the rhubarb [or apple] juice. If [desired, add] boiled and strained rhubarb or apple juice, pour the necessary amount of water [over them] and place it over the fire. Once it boils, throw in the meat, remove the foam, and throw in the ingredients (*masāleh*) according to the recipe.

Dried Fruit Āš

Sefat-e āš-e qure-ye xošk va zerešk-e xošk va zoqāl[9] -e xošk

All are cooked following the same recipe. Take dried unripe grapes, barberries, or cornelian cherries – whichever is desired – and boil and strain [their juice]. Cut into pieces fat hogget or lamb – whichever is desired –

8. *Rivāj* or *rivās* are the correct terms (rhubarb, rheum).

9. *Zoqāl*; short form of *zoqāl axte* (cornelian cherry).

and pound some (to make meatballs), too. Pour the necessary amount of water in a pot, [heat, and throw in the meat] and remove the foam. Pour whichever strained sour [juice] in it and throw in peeled chickpeas and diced onions. Throw in strip cut beetroot, and throw in the necessary amount of rice, celery, and diced mint. Throw in peeled shelled almonds and raisins and flavour with sugar. At the time it is to be done, add ground dried mint and pounded garlic and steam with the lid on for awhile so the aroma of the garlic is absorbed by it, [then] take [the pot] down and serve in a dish.

Fruit Paste Āš

Sefat-e āš-e rob-hā

Cook all paste [stews] – such as pomegranate paste, quince paste, unripe grape paste, apple paste, barberry paste, and cornelian cherry paste – according to the same recipe. Take fat hogget or fat lamb and slice it. Pour the necessary amount of water in a pot [and heat]. Once the water is heated, wash the meat thoroughly, [throw in the pot] and remove the foam. Throw in the necessary amount of chickpeas and diced onions. Throw in any [one] of the pastes that is wanted. Add large meatballs, beet, squash, celery, diced mint, and rice – the necessary amount of each – and cook. If it is wanted, add shelled almonds and raisins and at the time of taking down, [add] pounded garlic and dried mint and flavour with sugar and steam with the lid on for awhile, [then] take down.

Chapter Eight

On Harissa

Bāb-e haštom: Dar sefat-e harise-ye gandom va jo va harise-ye šir bā berenj va harise-ye maqz-e peste va morq va kolang va harise-hāye rangin

Wheat Harissa

Sefat-e harise-ye gandom

Take fat mutton, two *mans* from its leg, and a *man* of wheat. If more is wanted, [measure] as per this recipe. Then, pour the necessary amount of water in a pot [and heat]. Throw in the meat and remove the foam. Wash good, white, pounded wheat with warm and cold water a few times and throw over the meat. It would be better if the washed wheat was boiled in warm water in another pot so its murky water would be removed and [then] was thrown over the meat. Boil them together so it becomes thick and smooth and the meat becomes fall-apart tender. If needed, add water repeatedly. After that, remove the lid, stir with a ladle and remove the bones. If it needed [more] water, drizzle, and stir thoroughly with a ladle. Add enough salt and keep it warm. At the time of serving, heat good mutton tallow and pour over it and sprinkle [ground] cinnamon which would be good.

Barley Harissa

Sefat-e harise-ye jo

Take two *mans* of fat meat and a *man* of barley. If more is wanted, [measure] as per this recipe, and pour the necessary amount of water in a pot [and heat]. Once it is heated, throw in the meat and remove the foam. Wash well-pounded white barley six times with cold and warm water, throw over the meat, and boil so that it becomes sticky and stir with a ladle until it becomes quite sticky. Drizzle cold water constantly until the meat and barley cook. After that, strain the barley porridge into another pot and put the meat in the porridge, place on the stove, and kindle the fire. Once the porridge is brought to the boil, wash half a *man* of uncooked rice that has been pounded with salt and throw it in the porridge, boil, and stir with a ladle gently until the rice cooks and the meat becomes fall-apart tender. Throw in the necessary amount of salt, steam with the lid on, and stir with ladle in the morning. If it needed water, drizzle. If there was meat broth [to drizzle], it would be better. At the time of serving, pour fresh mutton tallow over it.

Rice and Milk Harissa

Sefat-e harise-ye šir ba berenj

Take three *mans* of fat meat. Pour water in a pot [and heat]. Once it is heated, wash the meat thoroughly, throw in, and remove the foam. Wash a *man* of white wheat and throw it in, or boil the washed wheat in another pot so its murky water is removed, then, wash with cold water and throw over the meat and boil until the wheat and the meat become fall-apart tender, drizzle water constantly and stir with a ladle until it becomes quite sticky and the wheat would not stick to the bottom of the pot. Once the porridge is done, strain it through clean thin muslin into another pot so that no wheat grain remains within the thick porridge.[1] Throw the meat in the porridge and place over the fire.

Once it is boiled, pound thoroughly the amount of three *čāraks* of rice with salt, cook, and wash with warm and cold water until it has whitened well. Throw it in the pot and boil until the meat, rice, and the porridge, all become fall-apart tender. Throw in some salt and steam with the lid on. Pour the amount of two *mans* of sheep's milk in a dish and keep in a cool place from the night before so it would not go sour. In the morning, strain that milk through clean muslin into a tin pot, place over the fire, and boil. Soak ten *mesqāls* of good [wheat] starch and strain it through clean muslin, and mix in the milk,[2] stir with a ladle, kindle the fire [underneath] until it is cooked well. After that, remove the lid of the harissa, stir with a ladle and take out the meat bones, stir with a ladle [again], and pour that milk as much as is appropriate. Follow the principles [of cookery] so it would not become [too] thick or thin, adjust the salt, and keep warm. At the time of serving, sprinkle some *Mahmudi* sugar that has been pounded with mastic over the harissa. It would be better if its (the porridge's) oil is almond oil, it would also be good to clarify fresh mutton tallow [and pour over the served porridge]. It would be better if it was served in a white china [dish].

This harissa is palatable and delectable. If it is wanted, add the meat, wheat and rice without milk. At the time of stirring with a ladle, if saffroned [harissa] is wanted, you must dissolve two *mesqāls* of nice-coloured saffron in water in a pot in which a *man* of wheat and three *čāraks* of rice have been cooked. After that, add some warm water [in the saffron mixture] and pour in the harissa, stir with a ladle, and adjust the salt. At the time of serving, it would be good if beef tallow was poured over it. If sugar was ground with saffron and was sprinkled on top of it, its colour would match [the colour of the dish]. If [desired, red] harissa can also be cooked as per the described recipe: [cook the porridge] with meat and wheat, remove [the wheat grains from] the porridge and add rice. At the time of stirring with a ladle, soak the amount of half a *čārak* of foxtail amaranth in warm water, squeeze through clean muslin, add in

1. Written 'strain it through clean thin muslin into another pot so that none of the thick porridge is remained within the wheat's grains'.
2. Written 'starch'.

the harissa and stir with a ladle, watching out for the [amount of] water so it would not peter out making it (the porridge) too thick. At the time of serving, pound a cinnamon stick soft and sprinkle on the harissa so it becomes tasty and colourful. It would be better to sprinkle ground mastic and sugar, too, and pour mutton tallow over it. Each of these [harissas] could have been described in different recipes, but to avoid lengthening [the manuscript], I attempted to be brief.

Rice Harissa

Sefat-e harise-ye berenj bi šir va san'at-e ān

Take mutton, three *mans*, it would be better if it was the meat of leg and pour the necessary amount [of water] in a pot [and heat]. Once the water is heated, wash the meat thoroughly and throw, in remove the foam, and throw in two *mesqāls* of cinnamon and a whole onion.

Once the meat becomes fall-apart tender, take out, strain the broth through muslin, wash its pot thoroughly and fill with the broth again. Pound one and a half *mans* of white rice with salt soft, sift through a sieve to remove its grits. Once [the broth in] the pot is boiled, wash the rice with warm and cold water thoroughly and add to the pot, the amount of water must be as much [as is needed for cooking] *šile palaw*.[3] Once the rice is half-done, shred the tender meat, throw in the rice, and stir with a ladle. If it needed water, drizzle, until the meat and rice come together. As cinnamon has been boiled within the meat, it needs not [to be sprinkled] on top of the harissa. At the time of steaming the harissa, add fifteen *mesqāls* of starch, dissolved [in water] and strained, to some warm and cold water, and add in the harissa, and stir for a few times together so they are mixed together, and steam with the lid on for a good while. Then, remove [the lid] and stir with a ladle. At the time of serving, throw in clarified fresh mutton tallow and if it is wanted, sprinkle sugar, which would be good.

3. See the recipes in Chapter Ten.

Pistachio Harissa

Sefat-e harise-ye maqz-e peste

Take [hogget], two *mans*, and pour three *mans* of water in a pot [and heat]. Once the water is heated, throw in the meat, remove the foam, and throw in the amount of three *mesqāls* of cinnamon and steam until the meat becomes fall-apart tender. After that, take [the meat] out of the broth, shred, and keep warm. Strain the meat broth and prepare the amount of a *čārak* of strained, soaked starch. After that, coarsely pound peeled, shelled, pistachios and wash a *čārak* of white starchy (*halim-dār*) rice thoroughly and pound. Skim the fat of the broth off its top as shelled pistachio is oily. Pour the amount of one *man* of water in a pot, [heat], add the coarsely pounded pistachio and the pounded rice both together in the pot, and stir gently with a ladle until they both are half-cooked. Throw in the shredded meat and stir with a ladle until they come together. Strain the soaked starch through thin muslin, add the amount of two ladlefuls of that broth, too, and pour a ladleful from the pistachio [harissa] pot into the starch so it would not become lumpy once it is added to the pot. Add it to the pot and stir with a ladle so they all mix together and steam like *šile palaw*. If its colour is [too] white, dissolve a little saffron – the amount of half a *mesqāl* – in cold water, throw in, and stir with a ladle. After that, powder some indigo in water, throw in, and stir with a ladle until it turns pistachio green and keep warm. At the time of serving in a dish, powder together some soft-ground shelled pistachios, *Mahmudi* sugar, and musk and sprinkle over the harissa. Pour almond oil or clarified fresh mutton tallow over it which would be good.

Hen Harissa

Sefat-e harise-ye morq

Take five large fat hens and one leg of mutton. Pour the necessary amount of water in a pot [and heat]. Once the water is heated, wash the hens thoroughly and with a knife scrape the lungs and liver of the hens off their back, wash thoroughly and throw in the pot. Remove the foam and throw in the mutton, too. Wash thoroughly one and a half *mans* of pounded white wheat four times with water and pour over the hens and boil together. If you boil the washed wheat elsewhere, remove its murky water, wash again with cold water, and throw it in the pot, it would be better and it would appear whiter. Boil until the hen and meat are done and the wheat becomes sticky. If the hens are cooked sooner [than the wheat and meat], take out. Boil the wheat and the meat and stir with a ladle until the wheat becomes sticky and would not stick to [the bottom of] the pot. Once the wheat porridge and the meat are done, strain the wheat porridge through a colander or clean thin muslin, and [press the porridge through the sieve with] the back of the ladle. Wash the pot thoroughly and pour the [strained] porridge in the pot again, throw in the mutton, and kindle the fire. Once the porridge is boiled, pound the amount of half a *man* of rice well with salt so it becomes whiter, wash it with warm water, add to the pot, boil, and do not stop stirring with a ladle until the rice is cooked. At the time of steaming, [put] the hens over the porridge and push them in [shallowly] so that they would not be submerged, add some salt, too, and steam with the lid on. At the time of stirring with a ladle, first take out the hens in a way that [any of] their small bones would not remain in the pot. After that, stir with a ladle, and remove the mutton bones as well and stir [constantly] with a ladle until it becomes as harissa should be. If it needs water, spoon warm water constantly, as much as it needs, and keep warm. At the time of serving, add mutton tallow and sprinkle ground cinnamon in it, for it would be good.

Goose, Crane, and Duck Harissa

Sefat-e harise-ye kolang va qāz va bat va san'at-e ān

All are alike. Take one and a half *mans* of mutton. Skin a crane and separate the crane's breast and legs. Pour the necessary amount of water in a pot [and heat]. Once the water is heated, wash the mutton thoroughly and add to the pot and remove the foam. Wash the crane's meat thoroughly, [boil] in a separate pot, remove the foam, and cook. Wash thoroughly a *man* of ground white wheat with warm and cold water four times and throw over the mutton so they boil together and become thick and smooth. It would be better to boil the wheat in a separate pot, remove its murky water, and [then] throw over the mutton.

Once the wheat porridge and meat are done, take out the crane's meat from the pot in which it was boiled, wash thoroughly with lukewarm water, and throw in the porridge, and boil until they all become fall-apart tender. Do not stop stirring with a ladle so the wheat porridge becomes quite sticky and would not stick to the bottom of the pot. If it is wanted, strain the wheat porridge through thin muslin and press through with the back of a ladle so that all the thick and smooth liquid is released from the wheat grains. Wash the pot thoroughly and add the [strained] porridge to the pot. [De-bone] the meat and crane's breast, there are some bones in the crane's legs; be quite careful lest them remain in the harissa. Wash thoroughly the amount of half a *man* of white rice that is pounded with salt and throw it in the porridge. Kindle the fire, boil, and do not stop stirring with a ladle until the meat, rice, and wheat porridge are cooked. Adjust the salt and steam with the lid on. At the time of stirring, spoon in water if it needs it, and stir until it is done, and keep warm. At the time of serving, pour mutton tallow over it and sprinkle ground cinnamon. The harissa of goose, duck, and crane are also [made with] this recipe, however, they do not need to be skinned, yet they must be washed thoroughly for it would be good.

Lamb Pilaf (*Qaliye Pilaf II*)

Chapter Nine

On Pilafs

Bāb-e nohom: Dar sefat-e palawdāne-hā ke čand no' ast

Lamb Pilaf - Qaliye Pilaf

Sefat-e qaliye palaw

Take two *mans* of fat hogget and dice it, say, larger than almond-sized. If more is wanted, [apply] this recipe: for each *man* of rice, [take] a *man* of fat meat, half a *man* of oil, and half a *man* of diced onions. [Wash the rice well and add it to a pot of boiling water and boil it until it is half-done, then drain the excess water.] After draining the [excess] water from the rice, [take] a *čārak* of peeled chickpeas, three *mesqāls* of cinnamon, two *mesqāls* of ground warm spices, and two *mesqāls* of caraway of *Kermān*, and add them all to the pot of rice as it would be good. Then, take two *mans* of diced meat and the necessary amount of water. [Pour the water in a pot and heat,] once the water is heated throw in the meat and remove the foam. Throw in the necessary amount of salt and throw in three *mesqāls* of cinnamon and a fistful of diced onions.

Once the meat is cooked, pound two and a half *mans* of rice with salt and sift through a sieve so its grits are out, wash it thoroughly, and throw it in a pot with half a *man* of peeled chickpeas [and enough water and heat]. Once the rice is half-done, drain the excess water if any, and throw half a *man* of diced onions, two *mesqāls* of caraway of *Kermān*, and two *mesqāls* of ground spices in the rice, with a *man* of clarified mutton tallow, toss from bottom to top, flatten the top of the rice, and steam with the lid on. Grind half a *mesqāl* of mastic in cold water and sprinkle [on top of the pilaf] and take down.

Lamb Pilaf - Qaliye Pilaf II

Sefat-e qaliye palaw – no'I digar

Take two *mans* of fat hogget and chop it almond-sized, salt, and let it be awhile so the salt is absorbed by its flesh. Take a *man* of clarified mutton tallow, add half a *man* to a pot, let it be [over the fire] and remove its foam and scum. Then wash the chopped meat thoroughly and fry in the oil. Then, throw in it a *čārak* of ringed onions so they fry together. Sprinkle some cumin and ground coriander in it and steam with the lid on. Pour some meat broth or clear water – the amount of five *mans* – in [another] pot. Throw half a *man* of peeled chickpeas and three *mesqāls* of cinnamon into the pot to boil. Pound two and a half *mans* of rice with salt to be well whitened and remove its grits. After that, wash the rice thoroughly with water three times and add it to the pot and boil until it is half-done and drain the excess water.

Quickly, throw half a *man* of diced onions, two *mesqāl* of ground spices, and that fried meat, all in the rice, and mix together. Throw in the remainder of the oil, too, and steam with the lid on. Douse the fire underneath it, grind mastic in cold water and sprinkle. If it is wanted for the topping of the pilaf, cook diced meat (*qeyme*) and meatballs with peeled chickpeas, onions, and warm spices. After serving [the pilaf] in a china [dish], sprinkle [the topping] over the pilaf.

Hen or Game Bird Pilaf

Sefat-e dāne palaw-e morq va kabk va dorrāj va kabutar-bačče va teyhuj

All are alike. Take fattened hen, francolin, or partridge, whichever is available, clean and chop. If squab or see-see partridge were available, wash them thoroughly. Pour the necessary amount of water in a pot [and heat]. Once the water is heated, wash thoroughly whichever [bird] that is available and throw in the pot with the necessary amount of salt, and remove the foam. Then, throw in a *čārak* of diced onions and three *mesqāls* of cinnamon so they boil together awhile. After that, take [the bird] out, wash with some salted water, and fry in oil. Strain its broth through clean muslin, and add it again to the pot, so that for each two *mans* of rice there would be five *mans* of water. Pound two and a half *mans* of rice with salt to whiten. [However,] if the rice was white, it need not be pounded. Boil the water, wash three *čāraks* of peeled chickpeas and two *mans* of rice thoroughly and add to the pot, adjust the salt, and boil. Once the rice is half-done, drain the excess water and throw half a *man* of diced onions and the fried bird – whichever [kind] there was – two *mesqāls* of caraway of *Kermān*, and two *mesqāls* of whole or ground peppercorns – whichever is desired – and mix together. Throw in a *man* of clarified oil and mix together and steam with the lid on for a good while. Grind half a *mesqāl* of mastic in cold water and sprinkle [over the rice] and serve.

Boiled Meat Pilaf - Yaxni Pilaf[1]

Sefat-e yaxni palaw va barri[2] palaw

[Both] are alike. Take fat mutton or fat lamb or fattened hen, whichever is available, and wash thoroughly. Pour the necessary amount of water in a pot [and heat]. Once the water is heated, throw in the meat and remove the foam. Throw in one diced onion and three *mesqāls* of cinnamon so they boil together. If boiled meat (*yaxni*) is wanted, let the meat cook thoroughly. If [you] wanted to fry it, take the meat out when it is yet to be fully cooked, wash with salted water and fry in oil so it is browned well

1. *Yaxni palaw* is a type of pilaf for which the rice is cooked in broth rather than water.
2. Perhaps misspelled '*barre*' (= lamb).

and strain its broth. The recipe is for every two *mans* of white rice, [take] one *man* of oil, two and a half *mans* of water, and three *čāraks* of chickpeas. Wash the rice and add it to the pot.

Once the rice is half-done, drain its water. [Add] half a *man* of diced onion, two *mesqāls* of caraway of *Kermān*, and two *mesqāls* of whole peppercorns. Whichever spice is desired can be thrown in. Throw in oil, toss from bottom to top, and steam with the lid on until it is done. Grind half a *mesqāl* of mastic in cold water and sprinkle, and place the boiled meat (*yaxni*) and the fried meat on top of the pilaf so it remains warm. Then, at the time of serving, first serve the rice in a dish, the meat in the middle, and rice on top of the meat again and if there was hen [instead of the meat, it should be served] as per this method.

Chicken and Caraway - Jamadi Pilaf

Sefat-e jamadi palaw

Take some fattened hens and wash thoroughly. Then, take peeled garlic, raisins, and a little amount of diced onions and stuff them and sew. Pour the necessary amount of water in a pot [and heat]. Once the water is heated, throw in the hen and remove the foam. Throw in cinnamon and diced onions. Once the hen is cooked, take it out, strain its broth through clean muslin and pour it back in the pot. For every two *mans* of rice, throw in half a *man* of peeled chickpeas, wash them thoroughly together, and throw in the pot and adjust the salt.

Once the rice is half-cooked, drain the excess water, throw in half a *man* of diced onions, caraway of *Kermān*, and warm spices according to the recipe that was described [earlier], and a *man* of clarified oil, toss from bottom to top and steam with the lid on. Grind half a *mesqāl* of mastic in cold water and sprinkle. Cut the excess fire underneath it (the pot) and place the hens on top of the pilaf so they remain warm. At the time of serving, first serve the rice in a dish, place as many hens as is wanted in the middle, again [serve] more rice on top so it appears good.

Mung Bean Pilaf
Sefat-e māš palaw

Take fat mutton or lamb, whichever is desired, and chop. Pour the necessary amount of water in a pot [and heat]. Once the water is heated, throw in the meat and remove the foam. Throw in the necessary amount of diced onions and cinnamon, [and boil] until the meat is cooked. If you cook a *man* of rice, clean half a *man* of mung beans and boil in another pot. Once the mung beans are half-done, take out, and sprinkle some salt. Strain the meat pieces (*qaliye*) and broth and add them back to the pot. Wash a *man* of rice as per this method and add to the pot. Once the rice boils and is half-cooked, wash the [half-cooked] mung beans and throw over the rice and mix together. Drain its excess water and add half a *man* of diced onions and half a *man* of peeled chickpeas as well which would be better. Pour in a *man* of clarified oil and toss from bottom to top and steam with the lid on. If it is desired, throw in the amount of a *čārak* of peeled garlic at the time [of] throwing in the rice which would be good.

Xoške Pilaf
Sefat-e xoške palaw va masāleh-e ān

Take two *mans* of good, white, unbroken rice and pound with salt and remove its grits. Pour four *mans* of clear water with the necessary amount of salt in a pot and boil. Wash the rice thoroughly three times and add to the pot. Once it is half-done, drain the excess water if any and steam with the lid on. If *kuku*[3] is wanted as its (the rice's) accompaniment, take ten eggs and crack in a dish with some salt, a *čārak* of diced onions, and a *čārak* of diced mutton (*qeyme*) that has been boiled in water. Mix some diced chives[4], some caraway of *Kermān* and five *mesqāls* of starch dissolved [in water]. Add a

3. An egg-based dish similar to frittata.
4. *Gandenā* or *tare*, a type of herb similar to chives.

čārak of good mutton tallow to the pan [and heat]. Once the oil is warmed, throw in the *kuku* [batter] and spread it on the pan. Once its bottom side is fried, cut [into pieces] and flip so the other side is fried, too, and keep warm. For *serkepič*:[5] take two fat young hens and cut into pieces. Throw the amount of a *čārak* of water into a pot [and heat] and throw in enough salt and chopped hens, and remove the foam and strain [the broth]. Add the amount of a *čārak* of good sharp vinegar, a *čārak* of ringed onions, and a *čārak* of mutton tallow and cook together so that the vinegar and water would peter out by the time the hen is cooked, and its oil appears. Keep it warm until serving the pilaf. If fried mutton stew (*qaliye*) is wanted: fry [the mutton] in oil and throw in onions and sprinkle vinegar.

If hen kebab is wanted: cook as per the recipe. If mutton loin kebab is wanted: split from the middle to double-cut double chops,[6] add cumin and coriander and grill. If meatballs are wanted: make from [pounded] mutton with onions and warm spices. If hen breast [patty] is wanted: [prepare] with onions and warm spices, and crack a few eggs in it and mix together. Spread on the palm [to shape] and fry in oil. If salted (smoked) fish is wanted: smoke in ash. If fresh fish is wanted: lay (the fish) in salt longer. After that, wash thoroughly and roast in a tandoor. All of these are accompaniments (*masāleh*) for *xoške palaw*. [For the] *āb-šole*,[7] pound unripe grape with fresh coriander and mint, and press [through muslin] and add some water so it becomes sweet and sour. Throw some ice or snow, and fresh cherry plum [...][8] like that. Prepare mint water, lemon juice, bitter orange juice or vinegar, whichever is available, as per this method. At the time of serving, serve *xoške palaw* in a china [dish]. Place *kuku* on one side, *serkepič* on another, the hen kebab on top, the mutton loin kebab on one side, and the fried-in-oil meatballs or fried meat (*qaliye*) [on another]. Serve all neatly in china [dishes] and prepare the *āb-šile* from whatever [juice] is wanted.

5. Literally: twined in vinegar.
6. Probably refers to a mutton loin double chop for which the cut is made from an unsplit lamb loin, and appears similar to two single loin chops.
7. Or *āb-šele* (extract or juice), might be a type of sauce.
8. A few words are missing here in the original manuscript.

Chapter Ten

On Sticky Rice

Bāb-e dahom: Dar sefat-e šile palaw ke čand no' ast

Sticky Rice

Sefat-e šile palaw

Take three *mans* of fat mutton, pound and make meatballs of half a *man* with onions and warm spices and chop two *mans* larger than almond-sized. Pour the necessary amount of water in a pot [and heat]. [Throw in the chopped meat] and remove the foam. Strain the chopped meat (*qaliye*) and broth again and throw in some diced onions and cinnamon so they boil together. Once the meat is done, wash two *mans* of rice and throw in the pot. Throw in three *čāraks* of peeled chickpeas and half a *man* of diced onions. Once the rice comes to a boil, [take] three *čāraks* of clarified oil [from which] first throw in half a *man*, and throw in half a *man* of chopped carrots, half a *man* of cabbage, two *mesqāls* of caraway of *Kermān*, two *mesqāls* of warm spices, and the small meatballs. Blaze the fire and stir with a ladle until the rice is half-done. [Then,] throw in the rest of the oil, beat with a ladle again, and throw in the spinach. At the time of taking down, grind mastic in cold water and throw in and steam with the lid on.

Sticky Rice II

Sefat-e šile palaw – no'i digar

Take two *mans* of hogget and chop it palm size as the meat for the *noxodāb*[1] recipe. Wash four fattened hens thoroughly and stuff the hens' cavity with cinnamon and onions. Pour the amount of six *mans* of water in a pot [and heat]. Once the water is heated, wash the meat and hens thoroughly, add them to the pot, [heat] and remove the foam. [Then,] take the meat and hens out, strain the broth, wash the meat and hens with lukewarm water, and [add] to the pot [with the strained broth]. Throw in a *čārak* of diced onions and three *mesqāls* of cinnamon so they boil together and adjust the salt. Once the meat is done, wash two *mans* of good, white rice and three *čāraks* of chickpeas together with warm water and add to the pot. Throw in half a *man* of diced onions, caraway of *Kermān*, warm spices, half a *man* of chopped carrots, and half a *man* of cabbage. [Take] a *man* of oil, throw in half a *man* with the rice and vegetables (*havāej*), blaze the fire, and beat with a ladle. Once the rice is done, throw in the spinach, and following the spinach, throw in the other half a *man* of oil, and blaze the fire. Once the rice is done to perfection, douse the fire. Grind some mastic in cold water and pour at the time of taking down and steam. Take the hens out [of the pot] before throwing the rice in and throw them back in at the time of taking the pot down so they remain warm. At the time of serving, first serve the sticky rice (*šile palaw*) in a dish, place two of the hens next to each other on top of it, and sprinkle some of the porridge and spinach over the hens. It would be good to cook diced meat (*qeyme*), meatballs, peeled chickpeas, diced onions, and warm spices separately[2] and serve over the sticky rice.

Hen or Game Bird Sticky Rice

Sefat-e šile palaw-e morq va dorrāj va kabk va kabutar-bačče va teyhuj

Take four fattened hens, wash thoroughly and chop them, for francolin and partridge, this method [applies] as well. [However,] if there was squab or see-see partridge, leave them whole. If there was a *man* of rice [to be cooked], pour the amount of three *mans* of water in a pot. If more is wanted, [measure] as per this method. Throw in the chopped hens, [heat] and remove the foam. Strain [the broth] again and add to the pot. Throw in a *čārak* of diced onions and a *čārak* of peeled chickpeas so they boil together. Wash a *man* of good, white rice thoroughly and add to the pot. Throw a *čārak* of diced onions again, caraway of *Kermān*, ground warm spices, carrots, cabbage, a *čārak* of oil, and small meatballs all [in the pot], blaze[3] the fire, and beat with a ladle so it becomes thick and smooth. When the rice is to be done, throw in the spinach. Throw in another *čārak* of oil and stir until it is cooked. At the time of taking down, grind some mastic in cold water and sprinkle. Cook francolin, partridge, squab, and see-see partridge, all according to the described recipe which would be good.

Lamb Sticky Rice

Sefat-e šile palaw be gušt-e barre

Take fat lamb, cut into pieces if it is wanted or chop if it is wanted. Pour the necessary amount of water in a pot [and heat]. Once the water is heated, throw in the meat and remove the foam. After boiling for some moments, take the lamb out and strain the broth and add [the broth] in the pot again. Wash the meat with lukewarm water and add it again to the pot. Throw in a *čārak* of diced onions and half a *man* of peeled chickpeas to boil for some moments. After that, throw in for two *mans* of rice one *man* of oil; half [of the oil] when throwing in the rice and [the other] half when [throwing] in the spinach, caraway of *Kermān*, and warm spices. Blaze the fire, and stir with a ladle. Once you have taken [the pot of] rice down, grind mastic in cold water and sprinkle it on.

1. See Chapter Five.
2. i.e. all together in another pot.
3. Written 'kindle fire' in the text.

Narcissus Sticky Rice

Sefat-e nargesi palaw

Take three *mans* of fat mutton and chop two *mans* larger than almond-sized and pound one *man* with onion and warm spices (to form meatballs). Pour the amount of five *mans* of water in a pot [and heat]. Once the water is heated, throw in the meat and remove the foam. After boiling for some moments, strain the broth and add it again to the pot and throw in a *čārak* of diced onions and cinnamon so they boil together. Then, make each meatball hazelnut-sized and put [aside] in a dish. Prepare all [of the following items]: a *čārak* of cleaned garlic, a *man* of carrots, a *man* of chopped cabbages, half a *man* of chestnuts, half a *man* of raisins, one *man* and a *čārak* of clarified oil, and a *man* of spinach.

Once the meat is done, wash thoroughly two *mans* of cleaned, white rice that have been pounded with salt with lukewarm water, and add to the pot. Wash thoroughly the small meatballs, half a *man* of diced onions, carrots, cabbage, garlic, chestnuts, raisins, and almonds, all and throw over the rice. Blaze the fire so it boils well. Throw in three *čāraks* of oil and stir constantly with a ladle and adjust the salt. Once the rice is half-done, wash the cleaned spinach and throw over the rice and stir. Pour in the rest of the oil and crack twenty eggs over the spinach, throwing each one in a [different] part, and sprinkle some ground salt over the eggs, steam with the lid on until the eggs and spinach are done. At the time of taking down, grind half a *mesqāl* of mastic in cold water and sprinkle. At the time of serving, first quarter the [layer of] eggs within the pot and take out and put in a dish. Then, serve the *nargesi* pilaf in a china [dish] and place the spinach and eggs over it so it resembles narcissus and that is why it is called *nargesi*.[4]

4. From and of *narges* (= narcissus); the finished dish resembles the flower with yellow center (yolk), white petals (egg white) and green stem and leaves (spinach).

Chapter Eleven

On Noodle Pilafs

Bāb-e yāzdahom: Dar sefat-e qabuli palaw va rešte palaw va jovak palaw va mānand-e ān

Qabuli Pilaf

Sefat-e qabuli palaw

Take four *mans* of fat hogget; chop one and a half *mans*, [cut] half a *man* palm-sized, and leave two pieces intact for pan frying (*tāve beryān*). Dice a *man*, add [the remaining] one *man* to a *čārak* of tail fat and diced onions, mix ground warm spices, and pound well [and form meatballs] so they would not fall apart [while cooking] in the pot. Then, pour the amount of five *mans* of water into a pot [and heat]. Once the water is heated, wash the chopped meat, two [intact] pieces of meat, and two cleaned young hens, and throw in the pot [and boil]. Throw in the necessary amount of salt and remove the foam.

[Take] the pounded meat and make small meatballs out of a *čārak* [of the mixture] and make three large meatballs out of a *čārak* [of the mixture] and stuff the meatballs with three peeled hard-boiled eggs. Then, throw the whole lot in the pot of boiling meat pieces (*qaliye*) and once they (the meatballs) set, take out quickly. [Take out the cooked diced meat] and fry the diced meat (*qeyme*) in oil. Take out the two pieces of meat that had been thrown in the pot of the stew (*qaliye*), smear with one [*mesqāl* of ground, dissolved] saffron and salt and fry in oil until well-browned. All [the rest of] the ingredients must be prepared before the meat and the fried meat pieces (*qeyme*) are ready.

First, cut three *mans* of white onions into thin rings, chop half a *man* of carrots into circular coins (*taneke*), chop half a *man* of cabbage into the size of *totmāj* noodles, and throw half a *man* of cleaned spinach in warm water [and boil]. Once it is half-done, take out, squeeze [the excess water out], and keep it warm, ready to be placed[1] [later] over the rice when the rice is almost cooked [to cook with the steam]. Add half a *man* of peeled chickpeas, a *čārak* of peeled almonds, a *čārak* of raisins, and, a *čārak* of peeled broad beans[2] if it is available, if not a *čārak* of shelled pistachios or a *čārak* of chestnuts, a *čārak* of peeled mung beans and enough lentils – both [mung beans and lentils must have already been] boiled. Then, take a *man* of maida flour and knead [the amount of] one dough ball of *rešte*, and one dough ball of thin *māhiče*, the amount of one dough ball of *zabāngonješk, jovak, omāj,* and *sarangošti* noodles.[3]

From all these ingredients (*masāleh*), any that is wanted can be used, otherwise use whatever is desired or is available lest it be [too] late.[4] Once the meat is done, take [the pot] down. Take out the meatballs after they were boiled for a moment so they would not overcook. Take out the diced meat (*qaliye*) and strain the broth in another pot and keep warm over fire. If it is wanted, add some oil and fry the diced meat. If un-fried (*nāberešte*) is wanted, [place] the boiled diced meat in the middle of the pot and round it, put the two fried pieces of meat, each on one side opposite the other and place two hens, each on one side [opposite the other], and fit [the rest of] the ingredients (*havāej*) and noodles (*ārdine*) properly next to each other. If coloured rice is wanted, clean three reed tripe with water and soap. Wash again thoroughly with water. At the time of setting the ingredients in the pot, take the amount of one and a half *čārak* of white rice, pour half a *man* of meat broth in a pot [and heat], wash the rice and add to the pot.

1. Written 'hide it in a corner'.
2. The seeds have been removed from the pod as well as the seed coats
3. See the recipes and the way to cut these noodles in Chapter Two.
4. i.e. use any of the named shapes of noodles or any other form you would rather before the time to add them is passed.

Once it has boiled for a moment, take down when the rice is par-boiled. Drain the excess broth, and divide the rice into three parts: For one part, soak some foxtail amaranth with a little water until it becomes quite red, squeeze and add [the red juice] to that rice. Stuff [one of] the reed tripe with that [red] rice, as much ground sugar suiting [the amount of] rice, and the necessary amount of oil, and sew its opening with a skewer or needle. For the two other parts; dissolve half a *mesqāl* of saffron in oil and throw in the rice, and mix together so it all turns saffron yellow. Separate half [of the yellow rice], add as much ground sugar that suits its (the rice's) amount and the necessary amount of oil. [Stuff the second reed tripe with it] and sew its opening.

[For] the remainder of the [yellow] rice, powder a broad-bean[5] amount of indigo and add to that rice so it turns pistachio green. Add the necessary amount of ground sugar and oil [to the rice and stuff the third reed tripe with it]. Wash these three [stuffed] reed tripe with boiling water thoroughly and place next to the [rest of the] ingredients (*masāleh*). The pot for this must be large so all the ingredients could fit. Place all (the ingredients) evenly next to each other. Wash two *mans* or three *mans* of rice – however much is wanted – and throw on the [layer of] onions. If it is wanted for the rice not to be blended with the onions, take cooked fatty *qālsun*[6] and a piece of mutton back and loin and throw in a pot [with water and heat] so it cooks while the ingredients are being cooked, too. Form the *qālsun* into a nice round shape, prick with a knife, and throw on [the layer of] onions [before adding the rice] so the rice would not be mixed with the onions, and throw the washed rice on that (*qālsun*). Some would also throw clean muslin on the [layer of] onions.

Cut a thin bread [round-shaped] to the size of the middle of the pot,[7] and fry both sides of it in oil as [you would for] noodles (*rešte*). At the time of throwing in the rice, sprinkle some warm water on it (the fried bread) so it becomes soft and would not break and place it over the onions, and

5. Used as a unit of measurement.
6. We were not able to find any definition for *qālsun* in different sources. However, we speculate it to be a layer of fat and thin meat, tripe, or intestine.
7. Caldrons have bigger bottoms and smaller tops; here, the author instructs to cut the bread the size of the middle of the pot so it is large enough to cover the layers of the ingredients that have already filled up half of the pot.

[before that] prick it all over with a knife, and throw over the onions. Throw cinnamon and warm spices over the ingredients (*masāleh*) before the rice. Throw in caraway of *Kermān* with the rice, pour the necessary amount of broth over and around the rice so that it covers the rice with two finger-widths [depth]. Drizzle half a *man* of oil along with the broth and blaze the fire so all parts of the pot boil. Once the rice absorbs the broth (*šarbat*) and oil, if it (the rice) is done, add the remainder of the oil; otherwise drizzle the necessary amount [of broth] and add the remainder of the oil and steam [with the lid on], and cut the fire underneath it, and let them (the rice grains) blossom.

When it (the rice) is done, grind some mastic with rosewater, sprinkle, and take down. At the time of serving, [mind that] it must be served in [three] large china [dishes]. First, remove the top [layer] of rice and place in a dish. Serve [a third of] that rice that is over the onions in elegant china. Then, remove the [layer of] onion that is over the ingredients (*havāej*) and place in a dish [and set aside]. After that, place enough of each of the other ingredient in a china [dish], serve again in the second china [dish] and add [enough of] the ingredients to that china [dish]. Again, [serve the ingredient in] another china [dish]. Up to three china [dishes] can be served accordingly. [Serve] the remainder of the rice in a china [dish] and sprinkle from all the ingredients over it. God knows best.

Qabuli Pilaf II

Sefat-e qabuli – no'i digar

Take three *mans* of hogget. Cut[8] one *man* palm-sized or larger than almond-sized. Pour the necessary amount of water in a pot [and heat]. Once the water is heated, wash the meat thoroughly and throw [in the pot] and remove the foam. Dice one *man* [of meat] and fry in oil. Pound one *man* (to make meatballs) and throw in the pot of boiling meat pieces (*qaliye*) until they set and take out quickly. If desired, cut into noodle strings (*rešte*) [dough that is made of] half a *man* of flour and fry in oil,

8. *Zaxm zaxm konand* (= stab, cut).

prepare [and set aside]. Then strain the broth into another pot and keep warm. Fry the chopped palm-sized meat with the boiled diced meat (*qaliye*) in *qabuli*'s pot[9] and spread out evenly at the bottom of the pot.

Prepare three *mans* of ringed onions and a *man* of peeled chickpeas, too. Put half a *man* of the [ringed] onions over the fried meat and put the fried diced meat (*qeyme*) over the onions, and again put half a *man* of onions over it with warm spices, and boiled small meatballs. Put half a *man* of onions over it, a *man* of peeled chickpeas over it and [another] *man* of onions over it, and [put] cinnamon in between and a layer of fried noodle strings (*rešte*), too, and [put more] onions over it [all].

Wash two *mans* of white rice thoroughly so you can pour over all evenly. Pour the broth over the rice all around the pot so that it covers [the rice with] two finger-widths [depth]. Blaze the fire so all parts of the pot boil. Some of (the rice) would remain uncooked if [just] one part [of the pot] is boiled.[10] Pour one *man* of oil in it in two instalments: half when adding the broth and half when the rice has absorbed the broth and [its grains have] blossomed. Adjust the salt of the rice properly and steam with the lid on. Cut the excess fire from underneath. At the time of taking down, grind half a *mesqāl* of mastic in cold water and sprinkle. At the time of serving, first serve the rice in the dishes. Then take out the ingredient (*havāej*) layer by layer and divide [equally among] each of the dishes for it would be good. If these ingredients – that were just named – are placed altogether in the pot next to each other with onions on top of all, washed rice on top of all, with the necessary amount of broth and the necessary amount of oil, this [method] would work, too.

Plain Qabuli Pilaf

Sefat-e qabuli-e sāde

Take two *mans* of meat and chop larger than almond-sized. Pour the amount of four *mans* of water in a pot [and heat]. Once the water is heated,

9. i.e. the main pot in which the pilaf would be assembled and cooked.
10. i.e. heat the pot evenly as the rice would not be properly cooked if the heat is not distributed evenly under the pot.

throw in the meat and remove the foam. Once the meat is cooked, strain the broth, and fry the meat pieces (*qaliye*) in oil in *qabuli*'s pot.[11] [Throw] two *mans* of ringed onions and half a *man* of chickpeas over the onions. Wash two *mans* of white rice thoroughly and throw over the onions and chickpeas and even [the top].

Throw in water over the rice, as per the [previously] mentioned method, as much that it stays two finger-widths (deep) above the rice. Kindle the fire so that it all boils well. [Add] a *man* of clarified oil: half when pouring the water, and half when it (the rice) has absorbed the water and oil and is [nearly] done. If it (the rice) is yet to be done, drizzle the necessary amount (of water).

After that, throw in the rest of the oil. Throw in some caraway of *Kermān* and cinnamon before [adding] the rice. At the time of taking down, grind mastic in cold water and sprinkle [over the rice], steam, and douse the excess fire. At the time of serving, first serve the rice on the dishes [then] sprinkle fried meat pieces (*qaliye*), chickpeas, and onions over all [of the dishes].

Rešte Pilaf

Sefat-e rešte palaw

Take three *mans* of fat hogget. Chop two *mans*, dice half a *man*, and pound half a *man* with warm spices (to make [both small and some large] meatballs). Then, pour the necessary amount of water in a pot [and heat]. Once the water is heated, throw in the [chopped] meat with enough salt, [heat,] and remove the foam. Cook the diced meat (*qeyme*) and [small] meatballs separately with onions and peeled chickpeas. Stuff the meatballs with three peeled, cooked eggs and throw in the broth.

Meanwhile, until the meat be done, make dough from one and a half *mans* of maida flour, cut into thin *rešte* noodles and fry in oil. Wash

11. Another pot; not the one in which the meat was boiled but the one that is going to be used to prepare the pilaf.

half a *man* of peeled chickpeas and a *man* of white rice thoroughly and throw in the meat base (*qaliye*). Once the rice is boiled for some moments, throw in the fried *rešte* noodles. Once the *rešte* noodles soften, drain its water immediately so that the rice and noodles would not overcook. Dice the amount of a *čārak* of onions and throw in with three *mesqāls* of caraway of *Kermān* and throw in a *man* of clarified oil all around [the pot]. Stir once with a skimmer so the oil goes down but the *rešte* noodles would not break. Steam with the lid on and douse the excess fire.

At the time of taking down, grind a *mesqāl* of mastic in cold water and sprinkle and take down. At the time of serving, push the *rešte* noodles to one side of the pot. Underneath (the noodles), first serve the rice in a china [dish] and then [put] the *rešte* noodles on top of it piling it higher in the middle of the china [dish]. Cut those egg-stuffed meatballs in half: place one piece on top and the three other pieces on three sides [of the dish]. Sprinkle the diced meat (*qeyme*), small meatballs, and [peeled] chickpeas – that had been cooked separately – on top of the *rešte* pilaf.

Rešte Pilaf with Hen

Sefat-e rešte palaw va morq

Take five cleaned, young, fat hens and cut into pieces. Pour the necessary amount of water in a pot [and heat]. Once the water is heated, wash the hen's meat thoroughly, throw [in the pot and heat], remove the foam, and strain the broth. Examine the hen's meat to make sure no feather is stuck to it and add to the pot again. Throw in a *čārak* of diced onions, a *čārak* of peeled chickpeas and five *mesqāls* of cinnamon to boil together. Pound half a *man* of meat with some tail fat, onions, and warm spices and make meatballs and add to the pot before [adding] the rice. Cut into thin *rešte* noodles [dough that is made with] a *man* of flour and fry in oil in a way that they would not break.

Then, pound three *čāraks* of white rice with salt, sift through sieve, wash thoroughly, and throw in the pot. Once the rice is half-done, throw in the *rešte* noodles so they soften and drain the [excess] water quickly. Throw a *man* of warmed clarified mutton tallow in it and stir with a skimmer from the sides of the pot so the oil reaches everywhere and the *rešte* noodles would not break. If it is desired, heat one and a half *mans* of sugar or one and a half *mans* of clarified honey and throw it on the *rešte* noodles and rice once the rice is done. It would have been better if the hen's meat was fried in oil [after boiling]. If it is wanted for the *rešte* dough [to be colourful], divide a *man* of flour into four parts at the time of making the dough. For a quarter (*čārak*) [of the flour], dissolve some saffron in water and the necessary amount of salt and make a good firm dough, cut into thin strings (*rešte*) and fry in a cauldron of oil trying to take out the noodles whole and unbroken. Green a quarter [of the dough] with saffron and indigo or with beet juice or spinach juice, make firm dough, cut into *rešte* and fry in oil. Make a quarter into white dough and cut into *rešte*, and make dough with a quarter [of the flour] and foxtail amaranth's water, cut into *rešte*, and fry in oil.

Once all these four coloured *rešte* noodles are fried, wash the amount of three *čāraks* of rice and throw it in the pot of the hen broth. Throw in the chickpeas and diced onions that were mentioned [earlier]. Once the rice boils for some moments and is half-done, throw in the [fried] noodles. Once the noodles have softened, drain the water immediately so they would not overcook. Pour a *man* of warm clarified oil in it and stir with a skimmer so the noodles would not break. Steam for awhile until the rice and noodles are done. As it was described [earlier], pour one and a half *man* of foam-free sugar [syrup] or warmed honey over it, and stir with the skimmer from all sides. Add some mastic, ambergris, or rosewater.

If it is wanted, cook diced meat (*qeyme*) and small meatballs with peeled chickpeas and warm spices. Sprinkle the amount of a *čārak* of spinach over the diced meat and mix with the diced meat. Out of fifteen eggs; crack seven in a bowl and mix together with the necessary amount of salt, a *čārak* of diced onions, two *mesqāls* of caraway of *Kermān*, and pour [the egg mixture] over each and every part of the cooked meat mixture (*qeyme*). Crack the remaining eight eggs and throw onto the cooked meat mixture (*qeyme*) separately, so it resembles narcissus. There must be as much water and oil in the diced meat strew (*qeyme*) that that spinach and eggs cook and the [liquid dries up and] oil reappears. Once it (the noodle pilaf) has been served in a china [dish], put a chunk of that eggy diced meat stew (*qeyme*) on the *rešte palaw*, and sprinkle ground sugar on top of it all, for it would be good.

Short-cut Noodle Pilaf[12]

Sefat-e jovak palaw va jušpare palaw va qušdeli[13] palaw

All are alike. Take a *man* of good, white flour and make a firm dough, knead [the dough well, pinch small portions out and form] into *jovak* noodles and throw [aside. Repeat] until it (the dough) is finished. Dry them in the shade and [then] fry in oil. Then, take a *man* of maida flour, make a firm dough, and spread it thinly, cut into *zabāngonješk* noodles, and fry in oil. Make dough from another man of maida flour, [spread thinly, cut into pieces and place the preferred filling on them] and bundle up to *jušpare* and fry in oil. Cooking these three would be the same way. Take two *mans* of meat; chop one and a half *mans* and dice and pound half a *man* (to make meatballs).[14] Then, pour the necessary amount of water in a pot [and heat]. Throw in the chopped meat (*qaliye*), [boil] and remove the foam, and strain. After boiling for some moments, throw in a *čārak* of diced onions and three *mesqāls* of cinnamon. While the meat is being done, fry the diced meat (*qeyme*), small meatballs, and peeled chickpeas in oil and drizzle [some water] until it is cooked. After that, wash thoroughly half a *man* of white rice with half a *man* of chickpeas with water and throw it in the meat broth. Once the rice is half-done, throw *jovak, qušdeli,* or *jušpare*, whichever is wanted, over the rice so they boil together for a moment [and steam with the lid on until the rice is done, then serve,

12. See Chapter Two for detailed instructions on how to shape these noodles.
13. *Qušdeli* is another name for *zabāngonješk* tree (ash tree) in some dialects. It seems these terms were used interchangeably in this recipe.
14. i.e. dice a quarter of the meat and pound a quarter to make meatballs.

and sprinkle the mixture of the braised diced meat, meatballs, and chickpeas on top].

Chapter Twelve

*

On Colourful Pilafs

Bāb-e davāzdahom: Dar sefat-e palaw-hāye rangin

*

Saffroned Pilaf

Sefat-e moza'far[1] palaw

Butcher four large fattened hens. Wash the hen's throat[2] thoroughly while it has yet to be scalded with warmed water. Insert a finger down its neck cavity and, using [your] fingertips, separate the skin from its back, breast, and crop enough that the finger could move through it. Then incise its belly and remove all the entrails and crop from the bottom, so that the skin of the crop remains intact. Wash the hen thoroughly with cold water and stuff it with fried diced meat (*qeyme*), peeled chickpeas, onions, cinnamon, and warm spices and sew securely. Crack sixteen eggs, four for each hen, in a dish and mix[3] together with some salt, a *čārak* of diced onions, and two *mesqāls* of caraway of *Kermān*. [Then] pour the amount of four eggs [of the mixture] down the hen's neck cavity and close the hen's neck cavity securely. Pour the amount of five *mans* of water in a pot [and heat]. Once it is heated,

1. = Coloured with saffron.
2. *Halq*: probably refers to hen's neck cavity. This was replaced with 'neck cavity' throughout this translation for ease of reading.
3. Written 'dissolve' in the text.

wash the stuffed hen with water again and throw into the pot and remove the foam. Throw in three *mesqāls* of cinnamon and a *čārak* of diced onions and enough salt so they boil together. Once the hen is cooked, take it out. Dissolve some saffron and salt [in water], smear the hen with it and fry in oil. Strain the hen broth and pound two and a half *mans* of rice with salt, sift, wash thoroughly, and add to the pot. Once it is half-done, drain the excess water. Powder two and a half *mesqāls* of good saffron in a little water and pour [over the half-cooked rice], pour the oil, too, and mix together until all turns yellow, and steam with the lid on. Once the rice is done, grind half a *mesqāl* of mastic in cold water and sprinkle [over the rice] and place the fried hens over it so they are warmed. To serve, first serve the saffroned [rice], place two fried hens on it and sprinkle some saffroned [rice] over the hens, too. Grind a *čārak* of sugar with some musk and sprinkle over the saffroned [rice].

Kallemāčān

Sefat-e kallemāčān

Take four [sets of lamb's] heads and trotters,[4] or however much is wanted, and remove the hair thoroughly with warm water, wash with cold water and dry and singe over the fire so any remaining hair burns. Wash again with pumice stone and warm water thoroughly. Pour the necessary amount of water in a pot [and heat] and throw in the cleaned head and trotters. Remove the foam and add enough salt [and cook overnight]. Once the morning arrives, first remove the fat froth and strain the amount of two *mans* of its clarified broth[5] into another pot. Then, take the head and trotters out and remove the meat of the head, tongue, and trotter's bones well, and place it (the meat) within the fat froth, keep warm, and adjust the salt. Add the amount

4. Each set of head and trotters consists of a head and four trotters.
5. i.e. skimmed broth.

of a *man* of water to the broth that was taken out of the pot and boil. Wash two *mans* of good white rice and throw it in that water[6] and adjust the salt. Once the rice is half-done, drain the excess water, if any. Pour two *mesqāls* of dissolved saffron and pour the amount of a *man* of mutton tallow, and the skimmed fat froth, all over the rice and toss from bottom to top so that the saffron colours all the rice yellow, let it be awhile until it absorbs the fat and blossoms. [Then] add the amount of two *mans* of warm clarified honey to it, mix together, and steam with the lid on until the rice is done. [Then] place the cleaned [and de-boned meat of] the head and trotters onto it so it is warmed. To serve, first serve the rice. Then, place enough of the heads and trotters [meat] on a china [dish] and sprinkle rice over it again and sprinkle ground sugar, too.

Yellow Pilaf with Jewelled Samosa

Sefat-e zard palaw ke ba morassa' bekešand

Take the amount of five *mans* of water and pour into a pot, [however,] meat broth would be better. Then, wash three *mans* of white rice thoroughly and throw it [in the pot and heat]. Once it is half-done drain its [excess] water. [Take a *man* of oil], powder three *mesqāls* of good saffron in cold water, add the amount of half a *man* of oil to it, and throw it in the rice, and throw in the remainder of the oil, too, and toss from bottom to top so that all the rice becomes yellow. Let it be awhile to absorb the oil. Add three *mans* of warmed clarified honey to it, toss from bottom to top, and steam with the lid on until the rice is done. Grind some mastic with rosewater and sprinkle [over the rice]. At the time of serving, [serve the rice and] place three yellow jewelled samosas over it – the way to make samosas will be described[7] – and sprinkle ground sugar with some silvered almonds over it.

6. i.e. the broth that was thinned with water.
7. See the recipe in Chapter Fourteen.

Red Pilaf with Red Jewelled Samosa

Sefat-e palaw-e sorx bā sambuse-ye morrasa'- e sorx

Take four *mans* of water and pour in a pot [and heat]. Once it is boiled, wash three *mans* of white rice thoroughly and add to the pot with enough salt. Once it is boiled, drain its [excess] water immediately. Warm a *čārak* of soaked foxtail amaranth,[8] and squeeze through thin muslin and pour into the rice and toss from bottom to top so that the colour reaches all over it. If [you] boil a *čārak* of foxtail amaranth in three *mans* of water, strain it, and wash three *mans* of rice with that [red] water and throw [all of it in the pot], it would be coloured better. Once the rice has absorbed the oil and the colour, pour three *mans* of warmed clarified honey in it, mix together, and steam with the lid on. At the time that the rice is done, take down. At the time of serving, first serve the rice in a dish, then place three red samosas on it neatly, and sprinkle ground sugar with some silvered almonds over it.

8. *Amaranthus caudatus*; also commonly known as love-lies-bleeding, tassel flower, or velvet flower.

Chapter Thirteen

On Sour Pilafs

Bāb-e sizdahom: Dar sefat-e siah palaw va limu palaw va qure palaw va somāq palaw va mānand-e ān

Black Pilaf

Sefat-e siah palaw

Take, say, three *mans* of fat mutton. If more than this is wanted, measure it as per this [recipe]. Pound a *man* of juicy, red pomegranate seeds and black currants[1] until soft, then boil the pomegranate seeds and currants in water. Heat three pieces of sour pomegranate rind and some iron[2] in the fire until red and throw repeatedly [in the boiling water with seeds] so it turns black, then strain through muslin. Once again, rub [the pomace] in water and strain again. Put the pot on the stove and boil the [strained] pomegranate juice again. Wash the meat thoroughly and throw it [in the pot]. Some [people] boil the meat and whole pomegranate seeds together to blacken the meat. However, throwing in [crushed and] sieved pomegranate seeds with the meat would be better.

1. Also known as Zante currants, Black Corinth, Corinth raisins, or currants.
2. A piece of iron would sometimes be heated and thrown into the stew, then taken out later. This apparently made the colour of the stew or juice darker.

Once the meat is cooked, take four *mans* of rice and wash a *man* of peeled almonds and one and a half *mans* of raisins and throw in the pot and adjust the salt. Drain the excess water if any. Pour two *mans* of oil and toss from bottom to top and let it be until the rice is done. When the rice is done, push the meat into the rice so it is warmed. At the time of serving, first serve the rice on the bottom [of the dish], then place the meat over the rice, and [serve] some rice again over the meat. If some peeled shelled almonds were to be boiled with some water and sprinkled on it when serving [it would be good]. Ground sugar would work, too. The method for [cooking] all sour pilafs is this way.

Lemon or Bitter Orange[3] Juice Pilaf

Sefat-e palaw-ye āb-e limu va āb-e nārenj

Take three *mans* of fat mutton and pour three *mans* of water into a pot [and heat]. Once the water is heated, throw in the meat and remove the foam, and strain. Add the meat and broth to the pot again and throw in half a *man* of diced onions and half a *man* of peeled chickpeas and boil together for [a] long [time], since onion cooks slowly in sourness. After that, throw in a *man* of lemon juice so it boils for some moments. Once the meat is cooked, take it out, wash three *mans* of rice and throw [in the pot]. Once the rice is half-done, try not to leave excess water so the sourness would not be spoiled. Add a *man* of clarified oil and steam with the lid on. Once the rice is done, place the meat on top of the rice so it is warmed. At the time of serving, first serve the rice in a china [dish], then the meat over the rice and some rice over the meat. It would be good if there was half a *man* of peeled shelled almonds and half a *man* of raisins in this pilaf of lemon or bitter orange and it was flavoured with sugar.

3. Also known as Seville orange.

Unripe-grape Pilaf

Sefat-e palaw qure

Take three *mans* fat mutton or fat lamb and cut to pieces and pour the amount of four *mans* of water in a pot [and heat]. Once the water is heated, throw in the meat and remove the foam. De-stem three *mans* of good large unripe grapes, wash, and throw over the meat so they boil together with the meat. Throw in one [piece of] stale bread to cut the bitterness of unripe grapes. Once the unripe grape is done, take down [the pot], and wash the unripe grape's pomace off the meat thoroughly. Then strain the unripe grape through clean muslin and throw [its juice] in the pot with the meat again, and throw in a *čārak* of diced onions and a *čārak* of peeled chickpeas. Once the meat is cooked, take it out. Wash three *mans* of white rice thoroughly and add to the pot. Once the rice is done, drain excess water if any, [but] try not to throw in too much water in the first place. Add a *man* of clarified oil and toss from bottom to top and steam. When the rice [grains] blossom, place the meat on top of the rice so it is warmed. When the time comes, serve as usual.

Sumac Pilaf

Sefat-e palaw somāq

Take half a *man* of good white sumac[4] and a *čārak* of maida flour. Rub half a *čārak* [of the flour] with sumac to whiten the sumac, pour a *man* of water in it, and soak together for awhile. Cut three *mans* of fat meat into pieces, and pour the amount of four *mans* of water in a pot [and heat]. Once the water is heated, throw in the meat, remove the foam,

4. There were no references found to what white sumac (*somāq-e sefid*) is called today. Sumac – as is known today – is a crimson red tangy spice made from grinding dried husk of red sumac drupes.

and strain. Add the meat and broth in the pot again, kindle the fire, and remove the foam once more. Add the sumac [mixture] in a [cloth] bag, hang, and place a dish underneath it so [its juice] is trickled in it. Dissolve some maida flour in cold water as well and pour in the sumac [juice] and mix together. Let it be [hanging] awhile so it is strained well, [then] pour over the meat. Sumac tends to foam; remove that, too, and boil with the meat until the meat is done. Then take the meat out, wash three *mans* of white rice thoroughly, and throw in. Once the rice is [half-] done, drain the excess water, add a *man* of clarified oil, toss from bottom to top, and steam for a good while. Once the rice is done, place the meat on top of it. At the time of serving, first serve the rice, the meat over that, and some rice over the meat again. If *šile palaw*[5] is wanted from this kind of sour pilaf (*torši palaw*), add some more water and throw oil and ingredients (*masāleh*) as per the recipe so it becomes sticky (*šile palaw*). Wisdom demands that any type of food that is cooked, is cooked well, orderly, and correctly, and not to spoil the ingredients.

5. Sticky rice; see Chapter Ten for recipes.

Chapter Fourteen

On Filled Pastries

Bāb-e chahārdahom: Dar sefat-e sambuse-ye morassa' va sambuse-ye sāde va qottāb va šakarbure

Jewelled Samosa

[Sefat-e sambuse-ye morassa'][1]

Take fat red meat, as much as desired, dice and fry in oil. Then, add diced onions and strained sumac juice or sifted ground sumac [mixed] with flour[2] [and heat]. [Once cooked], take down and add some ground cinnamon, cumin, and ground coriander. If plain fried meat filling (*qeyme*) is desired, add diced onion, ground pepper, cumin, and ground coriander. Take half-baked large, thin bread, fold over, cut a four-finger-width length off both its ends [to form a square] and fold over [diagonally] to form a triangle. Stick its side [together] with dough and stuff it with the filling (*qeyme*). Stuff the upper inner edge of the bread with the filling (*qeyme*) and attach its edge with dough to form a samosa. Next, for its jewelled topping, take two *mans* of good white maida flour with some salt and make a batter like *zolibiā*.[3] If saffron is

1. There is no heading for this recipe in the original manuscript.
2. Or can be read as 'powdered (*ārd*) and sifted ground sumac'.
3. See the footnote in Chapter One.

desired, dissolve two *mesqāls* [of it] in cold water and add [to the batter]. If green [batter] is desired, grind [saffron] with some indigo and add. Then, [mix] peeled shelled almonds, peeled shelled pistachios, and green raisins – as much as desired – with some of that batter. If red [batter] is desired, boil the amount of half a *čārak* of foxtail amaranth, squeeze [its juice out] and pour in that batter. For each samosa, cut two boiled eggs in half, grind a sugarloaf and prepare [and set aside]. Then, heat two *mans* of clarified oil in a large tub, coat the samosa with the batter of any colour and throw in that hot oil and sprinkle three fistfuls of that batter in the [hot] oil next to the samosa. Once the batter is set, take it out of the oil with a skimmer and place it evenly on top of the samosa. Place [some of] the shelled almonds, raisins, and shelled pistachios that have been mixed with the batter evenly on the samosa. [Take] the halved, boiled eggs, attach one in the middle and one on each corner [of the samosa] with the batter to the [rest of the topping] ingredients (*masāleh*). Quickly, sprinkle warm oil over the samosa with the skimmer so the top of the samosa is cooked thoroughly with that oil. Take care of the fire so the bottom of the samosa would not burn. Once it is cooked well, take out, and sprinkle [some] ground sugar.

Plain Samosa

Sefat-e sambuse-ye sāde

Take white red meat,[4] as much as desired, dice thoroughly, and fry in oil. Add plenty of diced onions and add sumac juice, or if desired, its powder. Add warm spices, cumin, and coriander. Take thin excellent bread, fold over, and a cut four-finger-width length off both its ends, cut again from the middle to the same size [shapes] and fold triangularly [to form a cone], secure its edges with dough and stuff it with necessary amount of the filling (*qeyme*), close its (the round cone) edge up over the filling (*qeyme*) and secure its edge with dough and fry in oil. If desired, eat it with sumac which would be good.

On Filled Pastries

Savoury Qottāb

Sefat-e qottāb-e varaq

Take half a *man* of white red meat and dice it until soft,[5] dice a *man* of onions, and add the necessary amount of salt, cumin, coriander, and ground pepper, too [and fry]. Then, take a *man* of fine white maida flour and make a firm dough, form into eighteen balls, and [spread] one by one smoothly on a stone [board] and smear hot suet over it so it becomes paper-thin. Place [each of the spread doughs] on top of one another. Do all as per this recipe. If round *qottāb* is wanted, place one [dough] on the bottom, spread the filling (*qeyme*) evenly on top of it, and place another piece of dough[6] over it, and stick the edge of both [top and bottom layers of dough together] and pleat its edge. As usual, pour some [melted] mutton tallow [in a tray] and place the *qottāb* in the middle of the tray, grease its top with mutton tallow, and place in the oven. At the time of taking out [of the oven], pour some warmed oil on it. If desired, eat it with sieved sumac flour. If wanted, take a big tub, and grease the inside of the tub with mutton tallow, and place the *qottābs* in the tub. Dig [a hole in] the ground the size of [the width of] the tub and [to] the depth of four-finger-widths. Burn much fire in [the hole] so it becomes quite hot and red, take the fire out, and place the tub in there. Place that burnt fire[7] in a griddle-pan that is the size of the top of the tub, and place it over the tub. Place some fire [that is burnt] in another place in the griddle, and let it be awhile [until cooked]. Lift the griddle once, if the top of the *qottābs* are browned, take them out. If not, let them remain for another while and take care of the fire [so it would not douse]. If the fire is inadequate, light the fire again, and tend until the *qottāb* is done thoroughly and take out.

4. Red meat that is pale in colour which is usually from very young animals.
5. i.e. mince the meat.
6. *Nān* (= bread)
7. i.e. burnt charcoal or firewood that is still hot.

Savoury Qottāb II
Qottāb – no'i digar

Take fat meat, dice, and fry in oil, and add diced onions and warm spices. Make a firm dough out of maida flour and make egg-sized balls. [Spread each of the dough balls] and put the filling (*qeyme*) in it. Fold [the dough] over, secure its edge [by pressing down the two sides together], pleat up, and fry in oil. This can be cooked while [staying] in the plains in where there is no oven. It can also be cooked in a tub, the way it was explained before; there is no need to repeat.[8]

Sweet - Šakarbure[9] Samosa
Sefat-e sambuse-ye šakarbure

Take a *man* of maida flour, one and a half *čāraks* of mutton tallow, and some salt and make dough. Pound half a *man* of peeled almonds, half a *man* of sugar, ground mastic, and a *čārak* of shelled pistachio and shelled almonds. Add sugar, knead together until they form dough, and sprinkle some rosewater. Shape the dough into egg-sized balls. Spread [each dough ball] on a smooth wooden board or a smooth stone [board], and fill it with [the mixture of] ground sugar, almonds, and ground pistachios. [Fold the dough over] and pleat its edge and pinch its top using a *menqāš*[10] to decorate. Dissolve some saffron in that [water] and smear on its top. [Or] soak some foxtail amaranth and squeeze the juice out and smear on its top, then decorate using

8. See the previous recipe for the instructions.
9. The pastry is commonly known as *qottāb* in Iran or *šekerbura* in Azerbaijan and is similar to Turkish pastry called *šekarpāre* (= piece of sugar, sweet piece; from Persian.
10. A *menqāš* is a serrated pastry crimper or a decoration tweezer used to decorate pastry surfaces.

Šakarbure Samosa

a crimper so it would look good. Put [the filled pastries] in the oven until cooked and tend to its temperature well so it would not overcook.

Chapter Fifteen

On Meat Stews

Bāb-e pānzdahom: Dar sefat-e qaliye-hā[1]

Abyssinian Qaliye

Sefat-e qaliye-ye habaši

Take three *mans* of fat hogget and chop larger than almond-sized. Then take half a *man* of pomegranate seeds and half a *man* of currants and pound them soft together and strain through a colander or thin muslin and add to a pot and boil. Wash the meat thoroughly and throw in with enough salt until it boils. After that, throw in ringed onions and peeled chickpeas and ingredients (*havāej*) such as a *čārak* of peeled almonds, raisins, black plums, dried apricots, figs, dates[2] – a *čārak* of each – and half a *čārak* of jujubes and boil until the meat is cooked. At the time of taking down, throw in pounded garlic and ground dried mint and steam, and then take down.

1. *Qaliye* is a stew where the meat is cooked with a little amount of liquid (often acidic such as verjuice, lemon juice, vinegar, etc.); the dish is drier than other meat stews, similar to braised meats or pot roasts, however, the meat is not necessarily seared first.
2. *Qasb*: a type of dry date known as *Zāhedi* which is yellow or light brown and not as sweet as other types of dates, it is grown in southern parts of Iran.

Kilwan[3] Qaliye

Sefat-e qaliye-ye Zangi

Take three *mans* of fat hogget and chop larger than almond-sized, salt, and let it be awhile. Chop some tail fat and fry in a pot. Then, wash the meat thoroughly, throw [in the melted tail fat] and fry. Throw in a handful of ringed onions and fry[4] together for a moment. Pound three *čāraks* of pomegranate seeds and half a *man* of black currants separately, and rubbing by hand, strain through thin muslin so that the pomegranate pomace would not pass through. Also, strain black currants while rubbing by hand through thin muslin. First, throw in the pomegranate juice to boil together [with the fried meat] and throw in one *čārak* of raisins. Once the pomegranate juice and raisins are boiled and the meat becomes fall-apart tender, throw in the juice of the black currants, and sprinkle [with] pounded shelled walnuts. Reduce the fire so it would not stick to the bottom of the pot, and stir so the currant juice and shelled walnuts reach its every part. Add pounded garlic and dried mint and steam with the lid on until its [liquid dries up and] oil appears and it becomes like *sangsir*.[5] At the time of serving, place a thin excellent bread in a china [dish] and serve the stew (*qaliye*) [over it]. It would appear pleasant if some silvered peeled almonds were sprinkled over it to decorate.

Pomegranate Seed Qaliye

Sefat-e qaliye-ye nārdān – no-e digar

Take three *mans* of fat hogget, chop two *mans* palm-sized and pound one *man* with one *čārak* of tail fat, onions and spices (to make large meatballs).

3. *Kilwa* Sultanate, a medieval sultanate founded in the 10th century centred at *Kilwa* (an island off today's Tanzania).
4. Written 'boil' in text.
5. The recipe for *sangsir* is called *sangbor* in this book; see the recipe in this chapter.

Then, take half a *man* of pomegranate seeds and half a *man* of currants, pound together, boil, and strain through muslin. Then, wash the meat thoroughly and throw in the pomegranate juice, and throw in half a *man* of diced onions and half a *man* of peeled chickpeas so they boil together. Throw in the large meatballs, too, and throw in a *čārak* of peeled shelled almonds, a *čārak* of raisins, and half a *čārak* of jujubes so they become plump, and throw in [some] diced fresh mint. Stuff two fat intestines with diced meat (*qeyme*) and diced tail fat, onions, peeled chickpeas, rice, and warm spices and boil in another pot and when they are almost cooked, take out and place in the pot of the stew (*qaliye*) so they absorb the colour of pomegranate seeds.

Once the stew is done, throw in pounded garlic and ground dried mint and steam with the lid on. At the time of serving, first take the stuffed intestines (*čarbrude*) out and place around a china [dish], then, [place] some pieces of meat and some large meatballs, and pour the pomegranate juice over the meat and stuffed intestines (*čarbrude*). Brighten [the food that is served] over the china neatly with oil and mint.

Sumac Qaliye

Sefat-e qaliye-ye somāq

Take the amount of half a *man* of sumac and a *čārak* of maida flour. Add half a *čārak* [of the flour] to the sumac, pour a *man* of water [over the flour and sumac mixture] and soak. Then, of three *mans* of fat hogget, chop up two and a half *mans* larger than almond-sized and pound half a *man* (to make small meatballs). If desired, chop the meat palm-sized and pour the necessary amount of water in a pot [and heat]. Once the water is heated, wash the meat thoroughly and add to the pot with enough salt and remove the foam. Strain the meat and broth again and place [the meat] in the pot. Then, [take] half a *man* of ringed onions, half a *man* of peeled chickpeas, and a *man* of chopped white beet.[6] First add the onions, then beets over

6. '*Salq-e sefid*'; could refer to turnip or sugar beet.

the onions, then chickpeas over the beet, then the small meatballs over the chickpeas, and blaze the fire. While the stew (*qaliye*) is yet to be done, throw the sumac in [a muslin] bag, strain it, add some maida flour again, and let it strain well, and blaze the fire [under] the stew. Once the onions, beets, and vegetables (*havāej*) are done, blaze the fire [under] the stew and pour the sumac [juice] around with a ladle.[7]

Once it is boiled, wash diced celery and squeeze so its dark water leaves and throw it [in the pot] until the stew is done. At [the time of] taking down, add pounded garlic and ground [dried] mint and steam with the lid on. It would be good if it is flavoured with sugar. If some pieces of bitter orange peel or dried lemon are thrown in the stew [while cooking], it would taste of bitter orange juice and become aromatic.

Lemon, Bitter Orange, and Mint water[8] Qaliye

Sefat-e qaliye-ye limu va nārenj va araq-e na'nā

Take three *mans* of fat mutton or hen and chop. Pour the necessary amount of water in a pot [and heat]. Once the water is heated, wash the meat and throw it in the pot and remove the foam. Then strain the broth and meat pieces (*qaliye*) and place again in the pot and pour as much water[9] to cover the meat pieces. Do not pour too much water so [the taste of] bitter orange or lemon juice would not peter out if there was little [of it available]. Then, once placed in the pot, place half a *man* of ringed onions, half a *man* of peeled chickpeas, and beet over one another, and small meatballs on top of all. Once the meat and vegetables (*havāej*) are half-cooked, throw in the needed amount of lemon or bitter orange juice and boil. Throw in [diced] celery and diced fresh mint. Throw in a *čārak* of peeled shelled almonds and a *čārak* of raisins, flavour with sugar, and steam with the lid on.

7. i.e. pour the sumac juice gradually all around the stew.
8. Mint water is not mentioned in the instructions.
9. Written *āb* (water) but it could also refer to the strained broth.

Unripe Grape or Cherry Plum Qaliye

Sefat-e qaliye-ye qure va āluče

They are alike. Take fat meat, say, three *mans* and chop. Pour the necessary amount of water in a pot [and heat], throw in the meat and remove the foam. Then, take the meat out, wash the broth off with some cold water, and place it in the pot. De-stem two *mans* of unripe grapes, throw them in water and boil, and strain through muslin over the meat pieces (*qaliye*). Add ringed onions, beets, squash, and peeled chickpeas over one another [in the pot]. Once the stew (*qaliye*) is half-done, [throw in] the small meatballs. Wash [diced] celery and diced fresh mint and throw [in the pot] and steam with the lid on. At the time of taking down, throw in garlic and ground dried mint. [Cook] plum cherry *qaliye*, according to this recipe, too; boil and strain [the plum cherries] over the cooked meat pieces and [add the rest of the] ingredients (*masāleh*) as per this recipe.

Rhubarb Qaliye

Sefat-e qaliye-ye ravās[10]

Take two *mans* of fat hogget, chop [one and] a half [*mans*] and pound half a *man* with onions and warm spices (to make small meatballs). Pour the necessary amount of water in a pot [and heat]. Once the water is heated, wash the meat thoroughly, throw in and remove the foam. Then, take the meat out, wash thoroughly, and place in another pot. [Take] the amount of four *mans* of fresh good rhubarb, peel its skin off, and cut to four-finger-width long [pieces]. Having pounded [the rhubarb], place it in a dish, pour some of that *qaliye* broth over it, and rub with [your] hands so the sourness is extracted from its body [to the broth] and squeeze through thin muslin.

10. = *rivās, ribās* (rhubarb).

Then, throw half a *man* of ringed onions, beets, celery, and fresh mint over the meat pieces (*qaliye*) and pour the strained rhubarb juice over it and boil. Once the stew (*qaliye*) is half-done, throw in the small meatballs and steam with the lid on. At the time of taking down, throw in pounded garlic and dried mint, and flavour with sugar.

Apple or Quince Qaliye

Sefat-e qaliye-ye sib va qaliye-ye beh

They are alike. Take fat hogget and chop larger than almond-sized. Pour the necessary amount of water in a pot [and heat]. Once the water is heated, throw in the meat and remove the foam. Strain the meat pieces (*qaliye*) and broth and place in the pot again. Add the necessary amount of water [or broth], half a *man* of ringed onions and half a *man* of peeled chickpeas over the meat pieces and blaze the fire. Once the stew (*qaliye*) is half-done, throw in the small meatballs. Once the small meatballs set, throw quinces or apples – whichever is desired – over the meat pieces and throw in celery and dried or fresh mint, and steam with the lid on. If the sourness is weak,[II] throw in verjuice, lemon juice, or mint water, whichever there was, and if it was [too] sour, flavour with sugar. At the time of taking down, throw in pounded garlic and ground [dried] mint.

Qaliye of Pastes

Sefat-e qaliye-ye robb-e anār va robb-e zerešk va [robb-e] zoqāl va robb-e qure va robb-e beh va robb-e sib

All must be cooked the same way. Take fat hogget and chop larger than almond-sized. Pour the necessary amount of water in a pot [and heat]. Once the water is heated, wash and throw in the meat, and remove the foam. Strain the broth and pour back in the pot again. The purpose of this straining of the broth is to observe well, lest there be any bits of bone, foam, or hair stuck to the meat. Then, once the meat pieces (*qaliye*) are placed in the pot, throw in half a *man* of ringed onions and half a *man* of pounded peeled chickpeas. Once the meat (*qaliye*), onions, and chickpeas are half-done, pour the necessary amount of paste – of any kind there is – on top of the stew (*qaliye*). Throw in peeled shelled almonds and raisins and throw in dried or fresh mint, flavour with honey or sugar, and steam with the lid on. At the time of taking down, add [ground dried] mint and pounded garlic.

Dried Apricot Qaliye
Sefat-e qaliye-ye qeysi

Take fat hogget and chop larger than almond-sized. Pound some too (to make meatballs). Chop half a *man* of tail fat, fry, and take out its crackling. Wash the meat thoroughly and throw and fry in [the melted tail fat] oil. Throw in a *čārak* of ringed onions and stir for a moment. Pour the necessary amount of heated water and boil. Throw in a *čārak* of ringed onions, half a *man* of peeled chickpeas, [some] small meatballs, and three *mesqāls* of cinnamon. Once the meat is half-done, wash one and a half *mans* of excellent, dried apricots thoroughly and throw over the meat stew (*qaliye*). The water must cover the dried apricots so the dried apricots could be cooked [well] and steam with the lid on so that the pot's steam would not escape and the dried apricots would thoroughly absorb a good amount of water, being on the one hand fall-apart tender [while remaining] firm on the other.[12] Once the meat and dried apricots are cooked [and their liquid dries up] and oil reappears, pour half a *man* of warm honey over the stew (*qaliye*) and steam with

11. i.e. to enhance the sour taste.
12. i.e. the apricots must be covered with water and cooked with closed lid so they stew in a way that their inner is thoroughly cooked yet they would not lose their shape.

the lid on so that the honey seeps through the core of the dried apricots. At the time of serving, place thin bread in a china [dish] and using a skimmer, serve the stew (*qaliye*) with oil over it. Sprinkle some silvered almonds with some poppy seeds and ground sugar on top of it and sprinkle [some] rosewater, too.

Twice the Onion - Dopiāze[13] and Pāšyarn[14]

Sefat-e qaliye-ye dopiāze va pāšyarn

They are alike. Take three *mans* of fat hogget and chop larger than almond-sized. Add the necessary amount of salt and let it be awhile. Pour enough water in a pot [and heat], throw in the meat, and remove the foam. [In another pot] fry the amount of half a *man* of tail fat and take out its crackling. Fry the cleaned[15] meat in oil and throw in a *čārak* of ringed onions and stir (and fry) for a moment. Drizzle from the meat broth to boil for some moments. After that, throw in a *man* of ringed onions, half a *man* of peeled chickpeas, three *mesqāls* of cinnamons, two *mesqāls* of warm spices, and throw small meatballs on top of the chickpeas and steam with the lid on. If *bāš yarn qaliye* is to be cooked, take twenty large, white onions, peel their skins and remove their roots with the tip of knife. Take the inside of the onion out from the root's place with the knife, like [carving with a] carving spoon. The cook (*bāvarči*) must always have such tools [handy] to be able to hollow out the inside of onions and squash easily. Then make meatballs[16] with

13. Literally 'with twice the onion'; this recipe seems different from the Indian *Dopiaza* or the dish that is local to Fars province in Iran.
14. Or *bāšyarn* as appeared in the next paragraph.
15. *Gušt-e kaf gerefte* (= the meat of which the foam has been removed).
16. There are three different forms of meatballs to be made here; one is to be used to stuff the hollowed onions, one is presumably larger and is stuffed with a hard-boiled egg, and the third is small meatballs. The stuffed onions are to be cooked with the diced meat as mentioned earlier in the recipe, the egg-filled meatballs are to be cooked in another pot and then added to the stuffed onions, and lastly the small meatballs are added with the rest of the ingredients.

diced onions, warm spices and pepper, stuff the onions [with them], and place on top of the meat stew (*qaliye*). Hide a few peeled hard-boiled eggs inside [the other] meatballs, cook them in another pot and place evenly next to the meatball-stuffed onions. Throw a *man* of thinly ringed onions on top of that with half a *man* of peeled chickpeas, three *mesqāls* of cinnamons, and warm spices. Throw small meatballs on top of all. Adjust the salt and steam with the lid on. At the time of serving, take out the onions, intact, and put on a dish and take out egg-stuffed meatballs, too. Set the ringed onions, small meatballs, and chickpeas aside in the pot and serve the meat pieces (*qaliye*) in a china [dish]. Then, put the intact [stuffed] onions on some spots [over the meat pieces].Then, cut the egg-stuffed meatballs in half and place on some [other] spots. Then, sprinkle a skimmer-full of ringed onions and chickpeas and small meatballs on top of it so it looks like a narcissus bouquet which would be good.

Carrot or Nargesi[17] Qaliye

Sefat-e qaliye-ye gazar va qaliye-ye nargesi

These are cooked the same way, but for *nargesi* eggs are added, and it will become *nargesi*. Take three *mans* of hogget and chop up. Chop half a *man* of tail fat, too – if desired – [and melt]. Throw the chopped meat (*qaliye*) in water, [heat,] and remove the foam, then fry in the tail fat oil. If it is desired, wash the meat pieces (*qaliye*) thoroughly, fry in oil, and drizzle broth or warm water, whichever that is available.

Once the meat is half-done, throw half a *man* of ringed onions, cinnamon, and warm spices in it. Throw one and a half *mans* of carrots on top of the onions, half a *man* of peeled chickpeas on top of the carrots, and small meatballs on top of the chickpeas and spread [the ingredients]. Boil until [all is] cooked and steam with the lid on. If it is desired, add half a *man* of warmed clarified honey. For *nargesi qaliye*, clean and wash the amount of a *man* of spinach, and once the carrots

17. See Chapter Ten for another recipe.

are half-done, sprinkle evenly over the carrots. Crack thirty eggs on top of the spinach one by one and sprinkle some ground salt and a little warm spices on top of the eggs and burn a fire [underneath] until the eggs are cooked and steam with the lid on. At the time of serving, first cut the spinach [and egg layer] into four pieces inside the pot, take out, and put on a dish. Then serve [the rest of] the stew (*qaliye*) and top the stew with that [divided layer of spinach and] eggs which would appear well.

Garlic & Yogurt Burāni – different types

Sefat-e qaliye-hāye burāni

Any *qaliye* to which garlic and yogurt are added is called *burāni*.[18] As it will be lengthy [to describe different types of *burāni*], all are described in one category, like beet *qaliye*, squash *qaliye*, aubergines *qaliye*, cabbage *qaliye*, cucumber *qaliye*, and spinach *qaliye*. All are cooked the same way. So, take, say, three *mans* of hogget and chop larger than almond-sized and salt. Chop half a *man* of tail fat, fry in a pot, and remove its crackling. Wash the chopped meat (*qaliye*) thoroughly and fry in that [tail fat] oil and[19] throw in a *čārak* of ringed onions and sauté for a moment. Then, add the necessary amount of broth or warm water. Do not pour too much so once the yogurt is added, it would not be tasteless, [but enough to] cover the fried meat pieces (*qaliye*). Once the water is added, for whichever stew (*qaliye*) there would be, throw half a *man* of ringed onions on top of the fried meat pieces.

If it is beet *qaliye*, clean [the beet] well, remove its root from its back, cut into wedges from the middle and chop evenly. If it is squash, clean [and remove] its inside and skin, and chop like [the shape of a] willow

18. This is the explanation widely used in modern day Iran, too. However, as stated by Perry in numerous researches on the subject (e.g. 2006), *burāni* was a dish made originally with aubergine for *Burān* (*Purān* in Persian), the seventh Abbasid caliph's – *Al-Ma'mun*'s – wife and daughter of *al-Hasan ibn Sahl* (an official and governor of Iraq, 813-833).

19. This sentence seemed redundant and was omitted: '[throw] one ringed onion. Or rinse the chopped meat (*qaliye*) with water and fry in oil'.

leaf.[20] If it is aubergine, peel its skin and prick some holes with the tip of the knife, or cut into four wedges, or cut in half from the middle and soak in salted water. At the time of adding [the aubergine pieces] to the meat pieces (*qaliye*), squeeze [out] the salt water, wash again with cold water and throw on top of the meat (*qaliye*). If it is with cabbage, trim its inner parts separately, divide the leaves, [chop up] and mix together and throw on top of the meat.

If it is cucumber or unripe Persian melon – whichever is desired – clean the skin and remove their seeds and skins. Throw in [either, or] both of these when the onions, chickpeas, and small meatballs have been added and the stew (*qaliye*) is to be done. Throw in cleaned spinach when the stew and the ingredients (*havāej*) are cooked, too. Wash beet, squash, aubergine, and cabbage thoroughly and throw on top of the onions and the meat pieces (*qaliye*), and throw chickpeas on top of that, and small meatballs on top of that, and boil until it is cooked. If soaked and boiled aubergines are thrown in the squash stew (*qaliye*), it would be better, and steam with the lid on. At the time of serving, add pounded garlic, strained yogurt, and dried mint [mixed] together. First smear some yogurt in a china [dish] and after that serve the stew (*qaliye*) in the china. Pour in a very little [amount of] water and [pour] yogurt in the shape of a square over it. Pour some [yogurt] around [the dish] and trickle some drops in the middle. Dissolve some saffron in oil and paint spots on the yogurt with the fingertips. Pour from the oil of the stew all over so its colour and proportion appears fine. Arrange neatly.

Lamb or Mutton Sangbor

Sefat-e sangbor-e gušt-e barre va gušt-e gusfand

Take lamb and wash thoroughly. Throw [in a pot of hot water] and remove the foam. If mutton is wanted, chop larger than almond-

20. A type of cut which resembles the willow tree leaf or the noodle shape with the same name mentioned in Chapter Two.

sized and boil more [than the lamb]. Then, take [the cooked meat] out and fry in half a *man* of clarified mutton tallow. Throw in the amount of a *čārak* of ringed onions, sauté for a moment, and pour a ladleful of the meat broth so they boil together and [the liquid dries up and] oil reappears. Throw also a *čārak* of peeled chickpeas [that have been] boiled elsewhere. Macerate the necessary amount of *kašk* [to make a] thick [liquid] and throw over the braised (*qaliye*) lamb. Pound a *čārak* of shelled walnuts well and remove [any remaining] bits of shell and clean it thoroughly and sprinkle over the [layer of] *kašk*. If there was much [water], drain it, and stir gently and slowly with the tip of a fork so it is boiled for some moments [until its liquid dries up]. Then, pound the necessary amount of garlic and dissolve in a little water and throw in. Throw in dried mint, too, and steam with the lid on.

Squash and Lamb Stew

Sefat-e qeyme kadu

Take a *man* of hogget, dice half a *man* and pound the half a *man* and fry in oil. [Then] add onions and peeled chickpeas. Drizzle [some water], throw in cinnamon and warm spices, and cook. Then, take three *mans* of squash, peel and clean the inside of the squash,[21] and cut the squash chickpea-sized or into thick strings and boil in salted water, take out quickly and let its water drain, fry in mutton tallow, and add to the meat stew (*qeyme*). Alternatively, chop the squash, wash it thoroughly and throw in the meat stew so that it cooks in the meat broth and oil. At the time of serving, pour over it pounded garlic [mixed] with strained yogurt and mint in the shape of squares and sprinkle some drops here and there. Mix dried mint together with the oil of the meat stew and drizzle over the yogurt.

21. i.e. scrape its seeds out.

✲

Fried Aubergine

Sefat-e bādenjān-e bereŠte

Take aubergines, [peel and] cut off their tops one-finger-width deep.[22] Using the tip of the knife, cut from where it has been cut [lengthwise from top] to its bottom on four sides and cut the sides of the aubergines [shallowly] and soak in salt[ed water]. Cut some [of the aubergines] into larger rings than [ringed] onions and soak in salted water so that its bitterness leaves its flesh. [Then] take out of that water and wash several times with unsalted water so that the salt leaves its flesh, squeeze gently and fry in oil.

Then, prepare diced meat and meatballs from mutton and fry in oil with onions, peeled chickpeas and warm spices, and drizzle (water) until chickpeas, onions, and meatballs are cooked and [their liquid is dried up] and oil reappears. Macerate *kašk* [to make a] thick [liquid] or strain sheep's yogurt and prepare [pounded] garlic and dried mint. Then, at the time of serving, first pour some *kašk* or yogurt in a china [dish] or any other dish there is and smear it all over it (the dish) with the back of a ladle. Place the aubergines [on the layer of *kašk* or yogurt] and pour again *kašk* or yogurt evenly all over the aubergines. Sprinkle fried diced meat (*qeyme*) and meatballs over it and place some rings of fried, ringed aubergines over the diced meat. Pour the *kašk* and yogurt – whichever is available – over it (the layer of ringed aubergines) and again, sprinkle fried diced meat over it. [The dish] would appear pleasantly colourful if some ground, dried mint was mixed with the oil of the fried meat (*qeyme*) and poured again over [the stew] and around the china. Drop yogurt on some spots, too. Dissolve some saffron with the oil of the fried meat and drop on top of the yogurt [spots] using fingertips, for it would appear better.

22. i.e. cut off its end to remove the stem end, positioning the slice one-finger-width below the base of the stem.

Fried Aubergine II

Fried Aubergine II

Sefat-e bādenjān-e bereŠte – no'i digar

Take as many aubergines as desired, cut off their ends and prick holes in them with a knife, and soak in salted water for awhile. [Then] take out of that [salted] water and wash with unsalted water, boil for awhile until they are cooked and take out quickly. Place [the boiled aubergines] in a colander and gently place something over them so their absorbed water trickles out. Heat the amount of a *man* of clarified oil in a pot and make batter with half a *man* of flour, dip the aubergines in it one by one, take them out, and let them be awhile so that the excess [batter] is trickled and [the battered layer on the aubergines] becomes flat. Throw [the battered aubergines] in oil and fry, then take out. At the time of placing them in a china [dish], add to it fried diced meat (*qeyme*), meatballs, and *kašk* or strained yogurt with garlic and mint.

Chapter Sixteen

On Roasts

Bāb-e šānzdahom: Dar sefat-e beryān ke čand no' ast

Roasted Mutton

Sefat-e beryān-e gusfand

Take fat hogget and roast [following the recipe below]. Separate the breast from the loin's edge and remove the shoulder. Remove the breast bone along with the neck and its bones. Remove the excess [parts of] leg and the spine and remove the pelvis. Wash thoroughly and salt. Wash thoroughly the amount of three *mans* of meat and throw in a pot with the necessary amount of salt, [heat,] and remove the foam. Then, throw three *mesqāls* of cinnamon and a *čārak* of onion [in the pot with the meat and cook] until they become fall-apart tender.

Fire up the tandoor. Throw [into the pot] the amount of four *mans* of rice [which has been] pounded with salt and washed with lukewarm water. Throw in peeled chickpeas, too, if desired. If saffronned [rice] is desired, dissolve four *mesqāls* of saffron [in water]. Once the [excess] water of the rice is drained, throw the saffron and oil and toss from bottom to top. If white [rice] is desired, drain the [excess] water as usual, and add a *man* of oil to two *mans* of rice. Toss from bottom to top and even the top of the rice [and steam with the lid on]. If wheat or bulgur is desired [instead of the rice], boil, and drain the excess water. For two *mans* of wheat, throw in half a *man* of oil. Fire up the tandoor well and put the rice pot in the tandoor. Wash the roasting [mutton] thoroughly, smear [it] with saffron or [damask] rose and hang over the rice.

If you are out in the plains, a griddle-pan must be placed above the tandoor with fire burning on its top, as the tandoor's temperature would not be right in the plains.[1] After awhile, open the side [opening] of the tandoor once and look [inside]: if it (the roast) is cooked well, take out. When serving, first remove the cow's butter[2] from the top of the rice and put aside. After that, serve [the rice underneath the butter] and place the butter on the side of the china [dish]. Place the good parts of the roast over the rice and place a skimmer-full of rice over the roast.

Roasted Lamb, Hen, or Goose

Sefat-e barre-ye beryān va morq-e beryān va qāz-e beryān va san'at-e ān

All are alike. The temperature of the tandoor must be burning hot. Prepare the lamb as per the recipe of the roasted mutton[3] and salt. Boil mutton and cinnamon in the water for [cooking] the rice [and when the meat is done], take the meat out, wash the rice, and throw in.[4] Once [the rice is] half-done, drain the [excess] water. Throw two

1. i.e. place a griddle-pan over the tandoor and burn fire on it to keep the tandoor hot enough for roasting the meat as the heat would leave the tandoor rather easily in open spaces.
2. *Kari-e gāv*; perhaps *kare-ye gāv* (= cow-milk butter); butter is served with the plain white rice that is to be eaten with roasts or kebabs in modern Iran.
3. See the previous recipe.
4. i.e. cook the rice in meat broth.

mans of oil for four *mans* of rice and put in the tandoor. Wash the lamb thoroughly, dip in salt, and hang on top of the rice. Blaze the fire of the tandoor [and the fire] on top of the griddle-pan so it is cooked thoroughly, and check [the doneness] by [opening] the side of it (the tandoor). Once it is cooked, take out and serve as per that (the roasted mutton) recipe.

Roasted Goose or Hen

Sefat-e beryān-e qāz va morq

Take some cleaned, fattened hens or fattened geese, wash thoroughly and add the necessary amount of salt so the salt is absorbed [by the flesh of the bird]. Burn a fire in a tandoor and [heat] the rice's water – if there was meat broth, it would be better – and once the water is boiled, throw in the washed rice. Once the rice is half-done, adjust the salt and drain the excess fire and [add] oil as usual. For two *mans* of rice, throw a *man* of oil, toss from bottom to top, even the top of the rice, and place in the tandoor. Poke [holes] in the hens' or geese's breasts with a fork and hang over the rice. Cover the top of the tandoor and place a griddle-pan on the top of the tandoor and burn a fire in the griddle – that is if you are out in the plains. If in the country, where the temperature of the tandoor is good [by itself, burning] fire on top of the tandoor is not needed until [the meat] is cooked. It is an absolute must to check the rawness or doneness of it (the bird) once from the side of the tandoor, and then take out. At the time of serving, put the cow's butter aside from the top of the rice, and serve the underneath [layer of] rice in a china [dish], place the chicken in between, the cow's butter on the side of the rice, and [more] rice on top of the chicken again.

Chapter Seventeen

✼

On Pan-Fried Meats

Bāb-e [hefdahom]: Dar sefat-e motanjane[1] ke čand no' ast

✼

Mutton Motanjane

Motanjane-ye gušt-e gusfand

Take mutton, say, three *mans*, salt it and let it be awhile. Pour the necessary amount of water in a pot [and heat]. Once the water is heated, throw in the meat, remove the foam, adjust the salt, and boil so that the meat is cooked. Then, take a *man* of clarified mutton tallow and add to [another] pot. Smear the meat with salted water and some saffron or dip in a little yogurt dissolved in water and fry in the oil so that both sides of it are browned. Sprinkle some water so it is entirely fried and cooked. If a plain [version] is desired, it is called pan-fried [mutton] (*tāve beryān*).[2] [It would be good] if half a *man* of ringed onions is thrown in so those, too, are fried [but] not for long. After that, [take] half a *man* of very sharp vinegar (*serke-ye qattāl*), pound a bulb of garlic, and mix together, and sprinkle on the meat and onions and steam with the lid on. At the

1. Literally: fried in skillet.
2. '*Tāve*'= pan, '*beryān*' = fried. i.e. the simple version is called pan-fried mutton which differs from mutton *motanjane*.

time of serving, take a few thin [pieces of] bread and lay them on the bottom of a china [dish], [place] the meat over the bread, and sprinkle a skimmer-full of [fried] ringed onions.

Lamb Motanjane

Sefat-e motanjane-ye barre

Take fat meat, cut to pieces and salt it, and let it be awhile. If the lamb was small, wash it raw and fry in oil. [However], if it was big, pour the necessary amount of water in a pot [and heat]. Once the water is heated, wash the meat and throw in with the necessary amount of salt and remove the foam. Once the lamb is half-done, take it out, and pour a *man* of clarified oil into the pot. Once [the oil] is heated, smear the meat with a little saffron or yogurt and fry in oil. Spoon water gradually [and fry] so its [liquid dries up and] oil reappears. If there was another pot, add some of that oil to that pot and fry half a *man* of ringed onions in the oil and place the lamb in it. [Take] half a *man* of good vinegar, pound a bulb of garlic, and mix together. Once the lamb is well-fried, sprinkle [the vinegar and garlic mixture], and steam with the lid on.

If [desired,] throw a ladleful of oil into a small pot and fry a *čārak* of ringed onions, [then throw in] some boiled chickpeas, a *čārak* of shelled almonds, a *čārak* of raisins, and some small meatballs, and some water and vinegar, flavour with sugar and [let it] boil awhile until its [liquid dries up and] oil reappears. Once the lamb is cooked, take some excellent thin bread, fold twice and knurl its edge. Spread one [piece of] bread over each china [dish] under the meat, place the meat over the bread evenly and sprinkle a skimmer-full of those ingredients (*havāej*) – onions, peeled chickpeas, almonds, raisins, and small meatballs – so it is adorned, and cover with a knurled bread.

Hen Motanjane

Sefat-e motanjane-ye morq

Take some hens, clean, wash, and salt. Pour the necessary amount of water in a pot [and heat] and throw in salt and the hens, remove the foam and boil until they are cooked. Then heat the necessary amount of clarified oil in [another] pot. Take out the cooked hens, smear with salt and fry in the oil and throw in the necessary amount of ringed onions. Once the onions and hens are fried, throw in some sharp vinegar and steam with the lid on.

Fowl Motanjane

Sefat-e motanjane-ye xorus bačče va kabutar bačče va dorrāj va taihuj

Take a cockerel and skin, wash thoroughly, and salt. After awhile, wash it thoroughly and fry in oil. If [desired], cook squab, francolin, see-see partridge, or sparrow in salt and water [then] take out and wash with salted water and fry in mutton tallow. Then, throw in the necessary amount of ringed onions and fry the onions as well.

Fish Motanjane

Sefat-e motanjane-ye māhi

Take good, fresh fish and scrape its skin[3] thoroughly and pull out all its entrails. Wash it thoroughly, add ample amount of ground salt, and let it remain in salt overnight. The day after, wash it thoroughly and cut it up

3. i.e. scales.

into slices. Add a *man* of clarified mutton tallow to pan and fry the fish well. Once it is taken out [of the pan], grind garlic and sumac until soft in some oil and rub it all over [the fried fish] so it turns red. If wanted, take the fish out of the oil, [then] strain the oil and pour some into the pot and throw half a *man* of ringed onions. Once the onions are fried, place the fish within the onions, mix a *čārak* of good sharp vinegar with crushed garlic, and sprinkle over it (the fish) and steam with the lid on so the garlic aroma does not leave it.

Chapter Eighteen

✻

On Offal Dishes

Bāb [-e hejdahom]: Dar sefat-e gipā-hā ke čand no' ast

✻

Hen Gipā

Sefat-e gipā-ye gušt-e morq

Take two cleaned hens and cut to pieces. Pour some water in a pot, wash the hen [pieces] and throw in [and heat] and remove the foam. Throw in three *mesqāls* of cinnamon and a *čārak* of small meatballs. Once the meatballs set, take out. Fry the hen meat in mutton tallow and [add] a *čārak* of diced onions, a *čārak* of peeled chickpeas, three *mesqāls* of cinnamon, two *mesqāls* of pepper and warm spices, and a *čārak* of mutton tallow. Then, stuff the tripe (*gipā*) with [the mixture of] fried hen meat, onions, chickpeas, spices, and the necessary amount of salt and add a *čārak* of clarified mutton tallow.

Wash a *čārak* of white rice thoroughly and take out of the water so that the water would not remain in the grains.[1] Then, powder half a *mesqāl* of saffron with a little water and colour the rice with saffron until it becomes completely yellow, add the rest of the ingredients (*masāleh*) to

1. i.e. the grains do not absorb much water and soften.

it and stuff the tripe (*gipā*).[2] If there are too much ingredients [left over], stuff two reed tripe[3] as well. Pour the amount of half a *čārak* of hen broth within the flat tripe[4] and adjust the salt. Stuff the flat tripe with the ingredients as well, pour the needed amount of water, prick [holes in the tripe] and tie with a string to a skewer, wash thoroughly, and throw in a pot [of water and heat]. Once it boils, take [the tripe] out, wash again, and shake so everything mixes together well and throw in the pot so its jacket[5] is cooked. Check [the doneness] by hand. If the rice appears to be soft within the jacket, take out [the stuffed tripe] and drain the excess water in the pot, and steam with some water until the rice [grains] blossom and [then] take out.

Mutton Gipā

Sefat-e gipā-ye gušt-e gusfand

Take sheep's flat tripe and clean it with warm water and wash thoroughly. Then wash thoroughly with soap a few times and again a few more times with water, [that is] a flat and a reed tripe. The recipe: there must be a *man* of fat red meat, a *čārak* of onions, a *čārak* of chickpeas, a *čārak* of rice, a *čārak* of oil, three *mesqāls* of cinnamon and pepper, and two *mesqāls* of warm spices. Then, dice [into] large [pieces] a *man* of fat, red meat and pour some water in a pot. Wash the diced meat (*qeyme*) thoroughly and boil slightly in water with necessary amount of salt. Then, take [the meat] out and add a *čārak* of diced onions, a *čārak* of chickpeas, a *čārak* of oil, and warm spices and adjust the salt. Wash a *čārak* of white rice thoroughly and add [to the mixture]. Stuff the flat and reed tripe and throw in the amount of half a *čārak* of the boiled, diced meat broth, secure [the stuffed tripe] to a skewer, and throw in a pot [of water and heat]. Having boiled

2. i.e. stuff the tripe with the mixture.
3. '*Širdān*' = abomasum; the fourth part of stomach compartment in ruminants, also known as maw and rennet-bag.
4. '*Šekambe*' = rumen; the first part of stomach compartment in ruminants.
5. Here the jacket refers to the tripe which has been stuffed.

for some moments, take it out, wash, shake, and add it to the pot again and cook. Take out once it feels soft to the touch.

Gipā II

Sefat-e gipā – no'i digar

Take a *man* of meat and tail fat, [dice into] large [pieces] and fry, or leave raw. Mix together half a *man* of [diced] onions, the necessary amount of salt, a *čārak* of [peeled] chickpeas, three *mesqāls* of warm spices, and a *čārak* of rice with a *čārak* of oil and a *čārak* of water and stuff flat and reed tripe. Prick [holes in the tripe], tie with a string (to a skewer), and place it in a pot [with enough water to boil]. Once it is boiled for a few moments, take it out, wash, shake, and add it again in the pot to boil. Once its jacket feels soft to the touch, take out.

Gipā III

Sefat-e gipā – no'i digar

Take the meat of loin and breast and chop into big [pieces]. [Stuff] two flat and two reed tripe with a *man* of [chopped] meat, half a *man* of diced tail fat, a *čārak* of peeled chickpeas, a *čārak* of oil, warm spices, caraway of *Kermān*, three *čāraks* of diced onions and the necessary amount of salt. Pour enough water so that the onion, tail fat, and oil are cooked in the water. Once it is boiled for a moment, take it (the stuffed tripe) out, wash it thoroughly, and add it again to the pot. There must be enough water to cover it. Steam as [you would steam] harissa,[6] cover the pot with lid and secure with clay. When it is to be steamed, prick [the tripe] with needle a few times so air does not remain inside and it would not crack open. At the time of taking out, remove it slowly so it would not fall apart.

6. See Chapter Eight.

Squash Gipā

Sefat-e gipā-ye kadu

Take three good squash, each of which weighing a *man*. Peel its skin thinly and scrape [and remove] its inside and wash thoroughly. Dice a *man* of meat and fry in a *čārak* of mutton tallow, throw in a *čārak* of [diced] onions, stir, and do so in a way that the onions would not overcook [or burn] and take down. Then, pour three *čāraks* of water in a small pot and boil. Throw in half a *man* of peeled chickpeas, half a *man* of small meatballs, and wash one and a half *čāraks* of white rice thoroughly and throw in.

Once [the rice] is half-done, drain the excess water, and throw in the fried, diced meat (*qeyme*), cinnamon, warm spices, a *čārak* of diced onions, and one more *čārak* of clarified oil. Mix [everything] together and stuff each of the three squash. Tighten the opening of the squash with dough and skewer to secure and place each in a metre (*gaz*) of clean muslin. Lift the four sides of the muslin and tie it tight so that the squash would not wobble in it. Boil all three squash in meat broth [in a pot] next to each other. If there was unripe grape meat broth,[7] it would be better. Boil until the squash cook, then take out, remove the dough from the opening, and place in a china [dish].

Sheep's Loin Gipā

Sefat-e gipā-ye pahlu-ye gusfand

Take [a whole-half] mutton and cut the entire piece from the back of its halved left loin as well as its halved breast to its neck.[8] Then, remove the shoulder bone and cut through its (shoulder bone) place reaching [to] the spine. Salt the inside and outside and let it be. Then, take half a *man* of

7. i.e. sour meat broth made of cooking meat in water and unripe grape.
8. i.e. take whole-half mutton and cut the entire meat from its loin, rib, and shoulder while keeping it intact.

meat, and add a *čārak* of tail fat, a *čārak* of diced onions, a *čārak* of peeled chickpeas, the necessary amount of salt, cinnamon, and warm spices and mix together and place in the shoulder's [deboned] space and stuff the loin. Sew [the opening] with a skewer or string, wash thoroughly, throw in the pot [and heat]. Remove the foam and boil until the meat is cooked. Then, place the whole [stuffed mutton] in a china [dish]. If desired, warm up the necessary amount of oil in a pot, fry it (the stuffed mutton) in oil so the meat is fried and the *gipā* stuffing is cooked too. It would be good to sprinkle some lemon juice.

Pot Gipā

Sefat-e gipā-ye dig

[*Pot gipā*] which is [also] called *soxtu be-dig*.[9] Take some young and fat flat tripe and clean it with warm water, then wash it thoroughly with cold water and soap a few times. Cook some slices of fat meat and flat tripe together until fall-apart tender. Then, take one and a half *mans* of meat, dice, and fry in a *čārak* of mutton tallow, throw in a *čārak* of diced onions [and fry] until they are both done. Then, strain the amount of one and a half *mans* of broth in a pot, boil, and throw in three *čāraks* of rice. Once [the rice] boils and is half-done, drain the water and throw in the fried diced meat (*qeyme*) with a *man* of diced onions, warm spices, and a *čārak* of oil in the rice and toss [everything together] and steam with the lid on. Cut the cooked flat tripe as the method for *totmāj*.[10] Once the rice is done, take a skimmer-full of rice, place the chopped flat tripe within the rice so that they are steamed together and [the tripe] is flavoured with the onion and spices. At the time of serving, serve the rice in a china [dish], the tripe in the middle, and rice on top of it.

9. In dictionaries *soxtu* is a type of dish, made with stuffing sheep's intestines. *Soqd* was a town near Samarkand (in today's Uzbekistan) and is mentioned to be the place where this dish originated. *Soxto* sometimes refers to sheep's or cow's tripe.
10. i.e. cut the cooked tripe into small squares similar to *totmāj* noodles. See Chapter Two.

Flat tripe Gipā

Sefat-e gipā-ye šekambe-ye barre

Cook meat and rice according to the recipe of squash *gipā* and stuff the flat tripe with it. Secure [the tripe's] opening with a skewer, throw in a pot and cook until the jacket of lamb's flat tripe is cooked.

Sheep's Čarbrude[11]

Sefat-e čarbrude-ye gusfand

If desired, stuff [the intestine], like *gipā*, with diced meat (*qeyme*), onions, chickpeas, warm spices, and rice, and throw in a pot [and heat] until cooked. If desired, boil a *man* of rice in meat broth with necessary amount of salt, drain its water quickly and take down. Then divide [the boiled rice] into four parts, each [mixed] with its [own] amount of ground sugar and oil: [colour] one with foxtail amaranth juice, one with saffron, let one remain white, and green with [a mix of] saffron and indigo. Tie the opening of the fat intestine and boil until it is cooked well. At the time of stuffing the fat intestine with rice, sprinkle some rosewater and mastic and arrange neatly.

11. Literally fat intestine; a type of *gipā* that is made by stuffing the intestine with fat meat and suet.

Chapter Nineteen

On Kebabs

Bāb [-e nuzdahom]: Dar sefat-e kabāb ke čand no' ast

Lamb Kebab

Sefat-e kabāb-e barre

Take a fattened lamb and butcher, wash thoroughly, salt it, and let it be. There are a number of ways to stuff it with [different] ingredients (*masāleh*). If desired, [take] pomegranate seeds or fresh pomegranates and ringed onions, chop maida bread and mix together with some oil, quince paste or barberry paste or unripe grape paste. If desired, pour some meat broth in a small pot and throw in [some] small meatballs, diced onions, and peeled chickpeas.

Once boiled, wash a *čārak* of white rice thoroughly and throw it in. Once it is boiled for a moment, adjust the salt, drain its water, and throw in some lemon juice and the necessary amount of oil. The recipe [for] *rešte palaw* or *qušdeli palaw*[1] – whichever is desired – is the same. So, all these could be used to stuff the lamb. Then wash the lamb again and skewer it, pass a thin skewer also from its back and truss the skewer securely with a string. Stuff its cavity with the ingredients

1. See Chapter Eleven.

– whichever is desired – and add sandalwood and rosewater and sew its stomach.

Kindle a fire and hold [the lamb over the fire from] afar so that the inside is boiled[2] and slowly spread the fire to its legs and shoulders. Once the legs and shoulders are done, spread the fire well all over it until cooked, and once it is cooked, sprinkle [some] lemon juice.

Hen Kebab

Sefat-e kabāb-e morq

Take some fattened young hens, wash thoroughly, salt, and let them be awhile. Then, take some pomegranate seeds with thinly ringed onions and stuff it (the hen), sew, and skewer. If desired, dice [some] onions and pound some pomegranate seeds, currants, shelled walnuts, and a little ginger. Add some sandalwood dissolved in rosewater to it (the pounded mixture), stuff its cavity and crop, and sew tightly with needle. Then prick [the hens] and cook slowly over the fire so that its crop would not burst.

Goose and Crane Kebab

Sefat-e kabāb-e qāz va kolang

If desired, stuff the crane either with *siah-palaw*[3] and pomegranate seeds or any desired paste. Or stuff [the bird] with pomegranate seeds, onion rings, cumin, and coriander. Then sew and skewer it and hold afar from the fire so that all its parts are boiled well [and roast]. Then sear over the flames until cooked.

2. i.e. keep the lamb afar so its meat cooks but its skin does not burn.
3. See Chapter Thirteen.

Meatball Kebab
Sefat-e kofte kabāb

Take the meat of young lamb and pound it soft with warm spices, onions, and the necessary amount of salt. Let it be awhile until it sets. After that, make large walnut-sized balls from it and skewer onto thin, flat, iron, skewers and cook over a gentle fire.

Vine Leaves Kebab
Sefat-e kabāb-e balg-e angur

Take lamb and some lamb's tail fat and pound [both] soft with onions and warm spices. Then, take fresh vine leaves that are quite sour. Stuff three vine leaves each with some of the pounded meat mixture (*kufte*), wrap, skewer, and cook over a gentle fire so that the leaves would not burn and the pounded meat mixture cooks.

Chapter Twenty

On Fried Meats and Patties

Bāb [-e bistom]: Dar sefat-e zonnāj ke u rā loqāne[1] guyand va šorāhi ke ān rā kabāb-e šāmi[2] guyand

Zonnāj Sausage

Sefat-e zonnāj ke ān rā loqāne guyand

Take, say, a *man* of hogget and half a *man* of tail fat. If it is the meat and tail fat of lamb, it would be more tender. Dice, but do not chop it too small. Mix together the amount of a *čārak* of onions, one and a half *čāraks* of maida flour or bulgur or rice flour, whichever is desired. Clean the hogget's or lamb's intestines and loosen the diced meat (*qeyme*) with the amount of half a *man* of water. Stuff the intestines [with the meat mixture] similar to small *loqāne*, flatten by hand and hang it for awhile so its water dries. Then, assort [the stuffed intestines] and fry in oil. Take them out and having set them in a china [dish], sprinkle [with some] sumac flour.[3]

1. From Arabic '*naqāneq*' or '*loqāneq*' (= sausage).
2. From *šām* (= Levant); of or relating to the Levant.
3. i.e. ground sumac.

Levantine Kebab

Sefat-e šorāhi ke ān rā kabāb-e šāmi guyand

Take the fat meat of young lamb, cut it thin and slice it to strips, salt and let it be awhile. Then, wash and fry in oil. If plain is wanted, throw in ringed [onions], cumin, and coriander. For those who eat it with honey, onion and cumin are not needed. Once it is fried, serve in a dish, and pour some honey over it.

Offal Qaliye

Sefat-e qaliye-ye puti[4]

Take lamb's head, trotters, flat tripe, and pluck. Clean all and wash thoroughly. Pour the necessary amount of water and salt in a pot and boil. Then take out, wash thoroughly, and fry in oil. Throw in diced onions and peeled chickpeas. Drizzle [some] warm spices [mixed] with water and pour some lemon juice for it would be better.

4. *Qaliye-ye puti* (also *Qaliye-ye pati* or *Qaliye-ye piti*) is a dish made by frying sheep or hen offal with onion. In some sources, '*put*' has been assumed to be synonym to liver.

Chapter Twenty-One

✲

On Tripe Soups

Bāb-e bist-o yekom: Dar sefat-e sirāb-e šekambe-ye gāv yā gusfand va jime[1]-ye gušt-e gusfand va qaliye[2]-ye puti-ye barre

Tripe soup

Sefat-e sirāb

Take cow's or sheep's flat tripe and wash them thoroughly. Wash them again with soap and leave them in salted water awhile, [then] again wash with cold water. Pour the necessary amount of water in a pot [and heat] and throw in the flat tripe with some pieces of fat meat to negate the smell of tripe. Once [the tripe] is half-done, take it out and wash thoroughly. Chop the tripe like large *totmāj*[3] pieces and place in the pot. Pour some of its topper [layer of] broth over [the tripe pieces] to cover and add some pieces of meat and boil until it is half-cooked. Then, throw in the amount of half a *man* of ringed onions, half a *man* of peeled chickpeas, and three *mesqāls* of cinnamon and steam until it becomes fall-apart tender. If desired, add lemon juice or strained sumac juice, sharp vinegar, and pounded garlic.

1. The pronunciation, meaning, and etymology of this word remains unknown to us.
2. *Puti qaliye* (offal *qaliye*) was the last recipe in Chapter Twenty.
3. See Chapter Two.

At the time of serving, throw in lemon or sumac juice to boil a little and throw in a *čārak* of peeled almonds, a *čārak* of raisins, pounded garlic and ground [dried] mint.

Offal mix
Sefat-e jime-ye gusfand

Take from all parts of sheep, say, a full *man* of loin meat and a *man* of breast meat, and the flank [should] not have been separated from the loin. Also, five sheep tongues, five sheep hearts, five spleens, five skirts,[4] a piece of the dark meat of leg,[5] five fat intestines, two flat tripe, five reed tripe and liver and lung. Wash all these thoroughly and add the necessary amount of salt. Wash the flat tripe thoroughly and wash again thoroughly with soap. Salt it [and let it be] awhile, too. Once all these are prepared, pour the amount of ten *mans* of water in a tinned [copper] pot and heat. Stir the hearts, tongues, and spleens [in the water]. [Tap] a little oil on suet and stuff the spleens with it and secure with a skewer. Wash all once again, throw in the pot, and remove the foam.

Once the meat is cooked, take out and wash with salted water thoroughly, and let it cool down and [let] the flat tripe cook well. Take out the rest once they are cooked and wash thoroughly and let them be awhile to cool down. First, cut the loins to triple-cut loin chops, then trim again, [but] do not detach from the loin.[6] Clean the tongues well and cut into round slices, cut the hearts into rings, shred the skirt meat, shred the dark meat, turn the spleens to the other side and cut it like *taneke*,[7] dice the livers and lungs, cut the reed tripe into rings, turn the fat intestine over and cut into round slices. Once the flat tripe is taken out [of the pot], cut into strings

4. Diaphragm, known as skirt.
5. *Siāhi-ye gušt-e rān.*
6. i.e. thinly slice the triple-cut loins but do not detach from each other (or the bone).
7. A type of coin, i.e. to cut the stuffed spleens to thin circles.

from its thin parts, and dice the rest. Boil the amount of a *čārak* of tail fat oil with its (*jime*'s) skimmed fat froth together until its oil appears.[8] Place all these [cut meat and offal] in piles in a tub, and pour from that warm oil all over, mix [the oil] with all and keep the tub warm over a fire. [Meanwhile] add a *sir* of pounded garlic and dried mint to a *man* of strained yogurt. Then, take some china [plates], and first, place two pieces of loins in the middle [of each plate] in the form of a square, and then put some from each [type of cut meat and offal] like piles at the sides of the china [plates]. Then, put half a spoon of the yogurt [on each pile], and drop some spots of saffron – that is dissolved in water or oil – on the yogurt. Pour the remainder of the oil in the tub all over it.

8. i.e. skim the fat froth and boil it with a *čārak* of tail fat oil and braise until its liquid reduces and oil remains.

Chapter Twenty-Two

On Sweets

Bāb-e bist-o doyyom: Dar sefat-e bāklavā-ye qarmāni va qeyre

Qarmān[1] Baklava

Sefat-e bāklavā-ye qarmāni

Take, say, twenty, thin, flat breads and a *man* of oil. If wanted, bake the bread the size of a pan and fry in oil one by one and take out. Once all (the bread) is cooked, remove the oil from the pan and wash the pan thoroughly. Prepare the amount of a *čārak* of boiled lentils. Place [each] fried bread one by one in the pan and sprinkle [some] of the boiled lentils, and [repeat for] another [fried] bread. Layer all [the breads and lentils] as per this method and [at the end] pour a *čārak* of oil over the bread, add a *čārak* of water to a *man* of honey and keep warm. Once all the bread is placed in the pan, pour the warmed honey, and place it over the fire and boil slowly until the honey is all absorbed by it. Place in a china [dish] that is wider in diameter than the pan over the pan and flip it quickly. Sprinkle shelled almonds, shelled pistachios, sugar, and ground musk on top of it and sprinkle [some] rosewater, too.

1. *Qarmān* or *Qaramān* is a city in today's Turkey.

Baklava II

Sefat-e bāklavā – no'i digar

Take two large trays and some excellent thin bread and size [it] to fit the tray. Then, melt a *man* of clarified oil in another tray and dip the thin bread, one by one, in that oil and place on the [other] tray. Sprinkle a fistful of sugar and ground almond over the bread. Dip another bread in oil [and place over the other one] and sprinkle sugar and ground shelled almond on it again [and repeat] until the tray is filled. Place another tray on top of it [to cover it] and place a coal fire underneath it so it boils slowly. Once the bottom side is [assumed to be] fried, lift the edge of the bread with the tip of knife to test, if it was fried, flip it in the [other] tray, and place over the fire again so the other side is fried, too. Pour some boiled sugar syrup over it so it boils and absorbs the syrup [so the liquid is dried] and oil reappears. Serve in a china [dish] and sprinkle some rosewater.

Baklava III

Sefat-e bāklavā – no'i digar

Take some excellent thin bread and a čārak of boiled lentils. Spread the bread, sprinkle some lentils over it, fold over each other, and cut into four-finger-width long [pieces] as per recipe of *barg-e bid*.[2] Pour oil in a pan, heat, and fry both sides of the cut [pieces of] bread, and remove the excess oil. Boil some honey or sugar with a little water and pour on it (fried bread) and boil slowly so [the sweetness of] the condiment is absorbed by it [and the liquid is dried] and oil reappears. Serve in a china [dish] and add sugar and ground musk over it and sprinkle [some] rosewater.

2. See Chapter Two.

Baklava III

Plain baklava

Sefat-e bāklavā-ye sāde

Take, say, two *mans* of bread and cut as [you would cut] *totmāj*[3] and fry in a *man* of oil. Pour a *man* of water [over the fried bread] and boil together. Then pour boiled honey over it. Once it is boiled for a moment, take down [from the fire] and sprinkle [some] rosewater.

Qatalme[4]

Sefat-e qatalme

Take white maida flour and the necessary amount of salt to make a loose dough (*dombe xamir*) and form into balls, each [weighing] a *čārak*, grease, and let them be awhile. Place [the dough balls] on a board until the dough [is rested and] becomes loose. Spread [the dough] and toss it in [your] hands, and if possible toss it over the shoulders so it becomes quite thin. Throw it over the board and smear oil all over it. Grease [each of the rolled out dough balls] and throw on top of one another. Heat an ample amount of oil in a frying pan and fry both sides [of the layered dough] in the oil, take it out, and pour honey over it. Or heat the honey and once [the bread] is out of the oil, throw it in the honey until the honey is absorbed, take out and sprinkle [some] rosewater.

3. See Chapter Two.
4. Or *qātlāmā*, a type of bread that is still baked in northern and eastern Iran as well as Afghanistan.

Čalpak[5]

Sefat-e čalpak

Take maida flour and make a loose dough (*dombe xamir*), grease, [divide] and make egg-sized [dough balls]. Spread [each egg-sized dough ball] on a greased board and fry both sides of it in hot oil, take out, and sprinkle [some] honey.

Completed with the help of God and His blessing
In 927 [AH (1521 AD)]

5. Or *čovak* or *čarbak* (literally: little oily thing) in Persian, or *Shelpek* in Central Asia, is a type of bread for which thin layers of dough are deep fried in oil.

Acknowledgements

We are indebted to all those who provided support, guidance and encouragement during this project, especially our families, without whom this work would not have been possible.

We would also like to express our sincerest gratitude and love to Iraj Hassibi, whose vast knowledge of Persian and Arabic classic literature helped us dearly throughout this translation.

The staff at the University of Tehran library have been remarkably supportive and helpful in facilitating our access to the original manuscript. We would also like to thank Catheryn Kilgarriff at Prospect Books, who was a pleasure to work with.

Finally, we would like to acknowledge the work of the renowned bibliographer and prominent expert in medieval and modern Persian manuscripts, the late Iraj Afshar who, among his numerous contributions to Iranian culture, modernised and edited Bavarchi's manuscript. It was he and his work that inspired us to pursue the translation of this manuscript in the first place.

Saman Hassibi & Amir Sayadabdi

Glossary

āb	water
āb-e gušt	meat broth
āš	thick soup or stew with legumes, grains or noodles
bādenjān	aubergine
bādie	large bowl
band-e qabā	long, wide, flat noodles
barg-e bid	short flat pieces of noodles
boqrā	flat disks of noodles
čārak	unit of measurement, equivalent to about 750 g
čini	china
dig, digče	pot, small pot
dig-e sefid	copper pot
foxtail amaranth	a plant whose leaves and seeds are cooked
gāz	scissors, tool
gaz	unit of measurement, equivalent to about a metre
gipā	tripe
harise	harissa
havāej	ingredients (see also *masāleh*)
hen	chicken
hogget	lamb meat form a yearling sheep
jovak	small barley-shaped noodles
jušpare	small filled noodles
kaf'	scum or foam
kafče	ladle or spatula
kafgir	skimmer
karbās	muslin
komāj	stuffed bread
komāj-dān	copper or earthenware cooking pot with lid
leng-e barre	large, flat fusiform noodles
māhiče	noodles
mahiče-ye bārik	flat, thin (and small) fusiform noodles
maida flour	finely milled white flour
man	unit of measurement, equivalent to about 2.75 kg

manto	a type of filled noodle
masāleh	ingredients (see also *havāej*)
māstbā	yogurt stew
mastic	resin of plant similar to pistachio plant
mesqāl	unit of measurement, equivalent to about 5 g
noxodāb	chickpea soup where *āb* is water
omāj	small thin noodles, similar t rice grains
palaw	pilaf
pulāni	large flat noodle disks with knurled edges
qaliye	chopped meat pieces
qāšoq	spoon
qeyme	diced meat, meat filling
rešte	long, thin flat noodles
rismān	string
sāj	griddle-pan
sangrize	small chickpea-sized noodles
sarangošti	small disk-shaped noodles
šarbat-āb dādan	to drizzle water
šarbati	bowl
sir	unit of measurement, equivalent to about 75 g
six	skewer
som-tarāš	paring iron
sumac	a tart spice from the berries of the sumac bush
šurbā	savoury stew
suzan	needle
tail fat	sheep with fat tails, baggy deposits on hind parts
tanur	tandoor
tašt	tub
toršipālā	colander
totmāj	flat squares (or circles) of noodles
zabāngonješk	long ellipse shaped noodles
zavāle	dough ball
zolf-e yār	twined pieces of noodles

Albala, Ken. 'Culinary history.' In *Routledge International Handbook of Food Studies,* edited by Ken Albala. New York: Routledge, 2013.

Ibn Sayyār Al-Warrāgh, & Nasrallah, Nawal (tr.). *Annals of the Caliphs' Kitchens.* Leiden, Netherlands: Brill, 2010.

Muhammad b. al-Hasan b. Muhammad b. al-Karîm, & Perry, Charles (tr.). *A Baghdad Cookery Book: The Book of Dishes (Kitâb al Tabîkh).* Totnes: Prospect Books, 2005.

National Consultative Majlis. (1933). Bill no. 92333, (18.10.1311 AH). (rc.majlis.ir/fa/law/show/92333?keyword). Retrieved March 10, 2016.

'Tenth United Nations Conference on the Standardization of Geographic Names.' July/August 2012. (unstats.un.org/unsd/geoinfo/UNGEGN/docs/10th-uncsgn-docs/econf/E_CONF.101_118_Rev.1_Transcription%20symbols%20for%20Persian_Updated.pdf). Retrieved April 5, 2016.

General Index

Recipe Index

Recipe Index